Landscapes of northern
PORTUGAL
a countryside guide

Paul and Denise Burton

SUNFLOWER BOOKS

First edition © 2004
Sunflower Books™
PO Box 36160
London SW7 3WS, UK
www.sunflowerbooks.co.uk

Published in the USA by
Hunter Publishing Inc
130 Campus Drive
Edison, NJ 08818
www.hunterpublishing.com

ISBN 1-85691-240-X

Traditional cork beehive (Walk 2)

Important note to the reader

We have tried to ensure that the descriptions and maps in this book are error-free at press date. The book will be updated, where necessary, whenever future printings permit. It will be very helpful for us to receive your comments (sent in care of the publishers, please) for the updating of future printings.

We also rely on those who use this book — especially walkers — to take along a good supply of common sense when they explore. Conditions can change fairly rapidly in this mountainous terrain, and *storm damage or bulldozing may make a route unsafe at any time*. If the route is not as we outline it here, and your way ahead is not secure, return to the point of departure. *Never attempt to complete a tour or walk under hazardous conditions!* Please read carefully the notes on pages 50 to 57, as well as the introductory comments at the beginning of each tour and walk (regarding road conditions, equipment, grade, distances and time, etc). Explore *safely*, while at the same time respecting the beauty of the countryside.

To Cassia and Natasha
Cover photograph: the espigueiros *at Soajo*
Title page: barrosā *calf and owner*

Sunflower Books and 'Landscapes' are Registered Trademarks.
Photographs: pages 22 (bottom), 25 (top), 26 (bottom), 29, 34 (top), 38, 40 (top), 44, 47 (top), 70 (top right), 72 (top left), 78, 80-81, 83 (top), 85 (top right and bottom right), 96, 100, 102-103, 108-109, 111, 120, 122 and cover: Brian Anderson; 39 (top two): António Jorge Barros, from the PNGP archives; all other photographs: Paul Burton
Maps: John Underwood
A CIP catalogue record for this book is available from the British Library.
Printed and bound in Spain by Grafo Industrias Gráficas, Basauri

10 9 8 7 6 5 4 3 2 1

Contents

Local interest panels

4 Landscapes of northern Portugal

☀ Preface

Northern Portugal — or more specifically, north*western* Portugal, is arguably the most beautiful part of the country. Here, in the province of Minho, the lush greenness of the coastal area, the Costa Verde, contrasts sharply with the exciting but stark and wild interior of the Peneda-Gerês National Park.

The very name Costa Verde ('Green Coast') is evocative — conjuring up images of a verdant landscape, and it does not disappoint. The vines for the famous *vinho verde* grow tall by the road, in the fields, in the mountains, up trees, up trellises, over pergolas, walkways and village streets — everywhere. Their fresh green leaves bring a vibrancy and texture to the countryside, which is stunning in its effect. Highly visible as

View from Cutelo to the village of Brufe and the granite peaks behind Covide in the distance (Short walk 5-3)

they are, the vines merely reflect the high fertility of this granitic region, and colourful meadows teeming with wild flowers vie with the grape for the visitor's attention.

In total contrast, inland Minho offers scenery of a mountainous nature and harbours the country's only national park, the Peneda-Gerês. Scenically beautiful and wild, where eagles soar and where wolves and wild boar still roam, it's one of Europe's last wildernesses. Sadly, the populations of these wild animals are now so diminished, especially the wolves, that they require protection.

If you explore with us, we can set your feet wandering over the hills into breathtaking scenic beauty. History still lives here, too, written millennia ago in the permanence of granite. Our walks follow some of the delightful old trails, built from huge granite slabs, which lead high into the mountains. You can only marvel at the effort and energy invested in their building, and wonder about the people who once lived in these mountains.

Many people in the Minho still live in isolated villages only recently connected to the modern road system, and some are still only accessible by foot; these villages are a delight to visit. It is like going back in time. The villagers vigorously pursue farming techniques developed four centuries ago and still largely unchanged. Long-horned oxen are central to the village economy — not just in the mountains, but also throughout the region. They are used both as beasts of burden and for food production. You may see them pulling ploughs in the field or the specially-designed carts along the road, often mingling with the traffic. There are many stories to tell, not just of the farming, but also of the culture, the famous *vinho verde* — and even of the region's wild flowers. Some of these stories are developed in the 'local interest' panels, the photograph captions and throughout the pages of the walks.

Walking is not the only way to explore this region, however. There is much to see and experience by following our car tours. Don't miss the Peneda-Gerês circuit, Car tour 3. After cascading down mountains, the river Lima flows sedately through a countryside which wholly reflects its majesty. The Lima Valley is surely the most beautiful valley in Portugal, and driving through it an unforgettable experience. Save time, too, for the other tours. The Vinho Verde tour will take you from the Lima Valley over to the Minho Valley, the whole route a never-ending sequence of terraced vineyards, sleepy villages and fine country estates. The Historical tour takes you to places you've already heard about — Bom Jesus, Citânia ... and many more. There is so much to see, in fact, that you may be content to relax with just a short walk and a picnic — so these have been highlighted in the touring notes.

The Romans believed that the river Lima was Lethe, the River of Forgetfulness. Anyone who crossed the river into the beauty of the south would forget his native land forever. You have been warned.

Authors' note

Our first association with the north of Portugal was in 1968 when we spent some 18 months involved in geological survey work. Through this we were able to visit many remote areas and villages — in those days still under the Salazar regime and truly isolated from the rest of Europe. Those 18 months whetted the appetite and opportunity arose and was grasped, in 1980, to move to Portugal to live. We were based in Viana do Castelo from where, almost every weekend, we would 'head for the hills' of the Parque Nacional da Peneda-Gerês in order to explore and walk.

Good maps were non-existent, literature on walks unheard of — and yet there was a wonderful network of old granite trails, still being used by local farmers, just waiting for walkers. Over a number of years we managed to piece together the jigsaw and link trails and paths into circular walks.

In the late 1980s we came across Brian and Eileen Anderson, authors of several Sunflower guides, as they sought to unlock the secrets of the area for a new book. We spent many happy hours with the Andersons, pouring over aerial photographs and showing them many of 'our' routes on the ground. As a result, a book on walks and car tours in the area was published for the first time.

We are still fortunate enough to be living in the area and, when it was suggested that we prepare an updated and expanded book for Sunflower on the area, we jumped at the opportunity.

Much on the ground has changed since the 1980s. Some of the old trails described in the original guide have fallen into disuse with rural depopulation and the increasing mechanisation of agriculture. But we have searched out several new walks, and there are now even some officially waymarked walks established by the National Park Authority and the local rural development agency, ADERE.

As a result, while much of the material in this new book is a revision and update of the original, we have rerouted many walks and taken the opportunity to add new ones. We wish to acknowledge with gratitude Brian's and Eileen's permission to use their text and some of Brian's excellent photographs.

— PAUL AND DENISE BURTON

Acknowledgements

Our gratitude to Brian and Eileen Anderson, whose original book inspired this expanded guide.

A special word of thanks is due to Dr Henrique Regalo of the Peneda-Gerês National Park Authority. His enthusiasm, ideas and comments, as always, helped us enormously.

Thanks too, to the staff at ADERE-PNPG and tourist offices in the area.

Tony and Annie Baker, Anthony and Linda Wilson all helped in checking the walks and re-walking them with us.

Finally our thanks to the Instituto Geográfico do Exército, for their permission to adapt their maps.

Recommended books

Most of the general guides to Portugal devote a chapter to the province of Minho and the Costa Verde. Worth reading are those in the Cadogan Guide, the Independent Travellers Guide (Collins), and the Rough Guide, while the Insight Guide is especially good for general background.

An excellent (and very inexpensive) bilingual series in three volumes published by Valima (the association of Lima Valley councils) is available in local tourist offices. This covers comprehensively the history, culture and geography of the Lima Valley.

For a thoroughly good read and in-depth view of the country, Marion Kaplan's *The Portuguese* (Viking, 1991) is strongly recommended.

For a highly readable account of Portuguese wine (with an excellent historical section which encompasses much more than just viniculture), *The Wines and Vineyards of Portugal* by Richard Mayson (Mitchell Beazley, 2003) is not to be missed.

Getting there and getting about

The north of Portugal is well served by the Sá Carneiro International Airport just north of Porto, with **daily flights** from many European cities including London and Manchester. But there are very few charter flights, and no budget airlines serve Porto. The airport is conveniently located for travelling north by road to the Minho and Peneda-Gerês, and all the major car hire companies have desks at the airport. Public transport north is more difficult, as one has to first go into central Porto — where there is no central bus station, and you will end up having to haul luggage around before catching one of the northbound buses.

It is quite easy to **reach the region by car**. If travelling from France (or arriving by ferry in Santander or Bilbāo), join the A52 motorway at Benavente and head west across northern Spain, passing Orense and carrying on almost to Vigo, finally heading south to enter Portugal at Valença. This may look a long way round, but until the long-awaited motorway linking Chaves to Vila Real is completed it represents by far the easiest driving.

Once in the region, there is a good **express bus system**, with frequent services to the major towns. This is useful if you want to travel from Viana down to Porto, for example, but the limitations of the **railways** (slow) and **local bus service** (see timetables pages 126-127) are soon realised when you want to explore the country regions. Buses do ply a route along the Lima Valley as far as Arcos de Valdevez, but beyond that private transport is required. **Taxis** are available in the major centres, but the distances involved to get you to the start of a walk could be long. In some cases, taxis could be used in conjunction with the bus, but you must arrange to be met for the return. Sharing a taxi with friends will obviously reduce the cost. **Car hire**, or **taking your own car** is, however, by far the best option for convenience.

Picnicking

On the following pages you will find some suggestions for picnics in the countryside, to enjoy while you are out touring (they are all keyed into the car touring notes and highlighted on the touring map with the symbol *P* printed in green). Take care where you park; don't damage the plants or flowers, and be sure not to block a road or track. It's a good idea to have stout shoes, a plastic groundsheet, and your sunhat to hand, if you are combining the picnic with a short walk.

Some especially beautiful picnic sites are to be found alongside the river Lima, and these are also accessible by bus (see  symbol and timetables on pages 126-127, but do remember to verify the timetables when you are in the region).

To help you find a picnic spot that appeals to you, we have included photographs of several settings.

Picnic food is widely available in supermarkets and smaller shops, as well as in the local outdoor markets. Some regional specialities are described on pages 19-23, where you'll also find details of market days.

1 Viveiro Florestal (⊓; photograph below; map page 60)
This shaded picnic site with tables and benches (and other facilities in season) is easily reached from Car tour 1 and lies very close to the start of Walk 1. On reaching the village of Montaria (see page 58), take a left turn signposted 'Viveiro Florestal' and then turn left again immediately (similar signposting). There is a car park 0.5km down this road. The picnic area is just over the bridge ahead of you. You can take a pleasant walk by following the river a short distance upstream, where you will find old watermills and lovely rock pools — a good place to 'get away from it all' if the main picnic area is busy.

2 Mézio (⊓*i*; map page 98)
This shaded picnic site with tables and benches (and other facilities in season) is accessible from Car tour 3. See page 96

(Walk 7) for details of how to get there. Park at Mézio (18.5km). The picnic site is on the right, just after you fork left onto the minor road. Nearby is a PNPG visitors' centre.

3 Santa Luzia, Viana do Castelo (⊓🚐; plan pages 130-131)
On the hill to the north of Viana (Car tour 1), the church of Santa Luzia stands impressively, looking down over the town. It is an interesting place to visit, not just for the church, but also for the panoramic views. You can walk up, but there are an incredible number of steps to climb (the route starts from the railway station and is signposted). If you are driving, follow Avenida 25 de Abril, the main through road, and then take the Estrada de Santa Luzia by the hospital, which winds its way to the top. There is plenty of parking space, and refreshments are available. Behind the church is a partly shaded picnic area and, beyond that, you can stretch your legs. There is an old, fairly large, Celtic settlement nearby; it is only a few minutes' walk up the road, on the approach to the hotel, over to the left. You will be charged a small entrance fee to gain access to the walkway designed to facilitate viewing.

4 Cais do Rio Lima (🚐; (photograph overleaf)
This partly shaded setting by the banks of the Lima is easily reached from Car tour 1. After Lanheses bridge (14.5km),

There are some idyllic pools and shaded spots just upstream from the Viveiro Florestal (Picnic 1).

look for a left turn at Vitorino das Donas, signposted 'Cais do Rio Lima' (18.2km). Turn left on this narrow surfaced road, and keep ahead at crossroads in 0.3km. Reach the *cais* (quay) in a further 0.3km and park. (From the Ponte de Lima underpass and roundabout, heading towards Viana, turn right after 7.2km). From the *cais* follow the track upstream to a Roman bridge, milestone and a short stretch of Roman road. Just over the bridge go left into a field, keeping round the field to the left and heading towards the river — up to 15 minutes on foot. By bus, use the Viana/Ponte de Lima service via Darque. Ask for 'Cais do Rio Lima' at Vitorino das Donas, then walk about 10 to 25 minutes.

5 Ponte de Lima (*i* 🅵 🚙; photograph pages 26-27; plan page 128)
Park as indicated in Car tour 1

(on page 25) and cross the old bridge to the opposite bank. There is a partly shaded official picnic site here, and a very pleasant park and garden as well. By bus it's a 10-minute walk from the Ponte de Lima bus station.

6 Santa Madalena, Ponte de Lima (🅵)
Perched on a hill to the south of Ponte de Lima (Car tours 1, 2) sits the small chapel of Santa Madalena. Occupying a superb position next to the chapel is a restaurant fronted by a large terrace, from where there is a fine view over the Lima Valley. Nearby is a shaded picnic site. Car tour 1 describes the route to Ponte de Lima but, to reach Santa Madalena, be sure to follow the by-pass. From this road look out for the signposted right-hand turn at a roundabout, taking care to turn right again 1.5km further on. As you approach the top,

12

This view across the river Lima was taken from just above the setting for Picnic 4. There are many such spots along this stretch of the river, most of them well signposted off the main road.

setting (no facilities), reached from Car tour 1 or 3. Park on the north side of the old bridge. The river is pleasant and clean for swimming, but deep in places. By bus use the Viana to Arcos de Valdevez service; alight at the old bridge.

9 'Bela Vista' — Bom Jesus (⩑; photograph page 29)
There is a partly shaded organised picnic site below this famous church. Follow Car tour 2, and turn left in 93.5km (signposted 'Bela Vista').

10 Casa Abrigo (map page 110)
Casa Abrigo is a secluded viewpoint in the mountains, overlooking the abandoned village of Branda da Bordença shown on pages 16-17 and 111. Follow Car tour 3; park at the 30km-point. No shade, but woods nearby.

11 Merindos (⩑*i*)
This is an organised picnic area (but with no shade) at a PNPG interpretation centre. Park as indicated in Car tour 3 at the 56km-point.

12 Adrão (⩑; map page 110)
This small picnic area, just by the church of Nossa Senhora da Paz is on the route of Walk 9. It is pleasantly shaded and has tables and benches. Follow Car tour 3; park at the 32km point.

the road divides three ways: take the middle route.

7 Ponte da Barca (*i*⩑🚐; photograph pages 32-33; plan pages 128-129)
An official riverside site (but *without* tables or benches), ideal for swimming and boating. Park as indicated in Car tour 1 (at the 43.5km-point). Then go down steps in the corner of the car park nearest the bridge, and walk under the bridge upstream as far as a chalet-type restaurant/café (about 5 minutes). There is little shade here. If you walk *downstream* from the bridge, you will find shade and picnic tables (but no swimming or boating). By bus use the Viana to Ponte da Barca service; get off at the old bridge.

8 Arcos de Valdevez (*i*🚐; photograph pages 36-37; plan page 129)
A partly shaded riverside

A country code for walkers and motorists

The experienced rambler is used to following a 'country code', but the tourist out for a lark may unwittingly cause damage, harm animals, and even endanger his own life. Do heed this advice:

■ **Do not light fires**; everything gets tinder dry in summer.

■ **Do not frighten animals**. The goats and sheep you may encounter on your walks are not tame. By making loud noises or trying to touch them or photograph them, you may cause them to run in fear and be hurt.

■ **Walk quietly** through all farms, hamlets and villages, leaving all gates just as you found them. Gates do have a purpose, usually to keep animals in (or out of) an area. Remember, too, that gates may be of a temporary nature, like brushwood across the path, but they serve the same purpose, so please replace them after passing.

■ **Protect all wild and cultivated plants**. Don't try to pick wild flowers or uproot saplings. They will die before you even get back to your base. When photographing wild flowers, watch where you put your feet, so that you do not destroy others in the process. Obviously fruit and crops are someone's private property and should not be touched. **Never walk over cultivated land.**

■ **Take all your litter away with you**.

■ Walkers — **do not take risks**. Do not attempt walks beyond your capacity and **never** walk alone. Always tell a responsible person exactly where you are going and what time you plan to return. Remember, if you become lost or injure yourself, it may be a long time before you are found. Remember, too, that **any route described here could become dangerous, due to storm damage or bulldozing**. On any but very short walks near villages, it's a good idea to take along a torch, whistle, compass, mobile phone, extra water and warm clothing — as well as some high energy food like chocolate. Please read carefully the *Important note* on page 2, our general advice about walking on pages 50-57, and our specific comments about grade and equipment at the beginning of each walk.

We came across this shepherdess near the top of Bicos (Walk 7) and witnessed the delivery of a newborn lamb. Somehow this just emphasised the timelessness of the enormous vistas in front of us and man's activity in these uplands.

☀ Touring

The Minho is still relatively unexplored and peaceful, hiding a wealth of interest. But be warned, distances can take much longer to cover than you would expect, due to the winding and indirect nature of many of the roads, especially inland where the recent road improvements seen on the coast have yet to arrive. The road surfaces themselves are on the whole fairly good, even the few remaining old cobbled stretches.

If you are hiring a car in Porto, the drive north is fairly straightforward, since the airport is on the north side of the city. From Porto to Viana do Castelo the new IC1 highway has greatly simplified getting to the area. The A3 toll motorway from Porto to Braga/Ponte de Lima/Valença also provides excellent access to the more inland parts. Avoid Porto and Viana at peak travelling times if possible — especially Porto, where you can expect constant traffic jams (a point to bear in mind if there's a flight to catch).

The inland road network in the north is adequately signposted, and the road surfaces are generally quite good. A new road from Viana to Ponte de Lima, Arcos and Ponte da Barca is already partly open; once complete, this will transform access up the Lima Valley.

Maps do not always show minor roads or tracks — especially in the more remote areas. The touring map in this book indicates main roads, other roads used in the tours, and tracks that are considered suitable for rental cars. Should you require a more detailed map, the 'ForWays' Minho map (available at Porto airport) is good for following the main routes and has good street maps of Viana and Braga. Turinta publish an excellent series of maps of Portugal and have specific sheets for the north and Porto. The excellent Northern Area map published by the Automóvel Club de Portugal (the Portuguese 'AA') is extremely detailed and kept well up-to-date.

It is usually cheaper to arrange and pay for **car hire** through one of the main hire companies before you leave home, but shop around. There are also excellent fly/drive offers, especially outside the main tourist season.

Take care when renting; before setting out check the car (have you got a spare tyre, jack, enough petrol, etc?), and clarify the rental conditions and insurance coverage. Take time, however tedious, to read the terms of the agreement. It is imperative to ensure that 'collision damage waiver' (CDW) is included in the insurance, to cover damage to your hire car if repair costs cannot be recovered from a third party. Tyre and windscreen damage are the responsibility of the hirer (including punctures), so check carefully before you drive off — including the spare. Don't hesitate to refuse a car if you're not happy with it. Always carry the agency's phone number with you, and take some water, food and warm clothing in case of breakdown. The wearing of seat belts is compulsory, and the local people comply outside the main towns — but there seems to be some unspoken agreement that they aren't necessary in built-up areas. Always wear your seat belt!

New **service areas** have been opened on the IC1 just to the north of Porto and to the south of Viana. The A3 has two service areas between Porto and Valença. **Petrol** stations are fairly frequent along the main roads, but there are only the occasional petrol stations in country areas, beyond Arcos and Ponte da Barca. If you are heading inland, go with a full tank of petrol. Some

grades of petrol may be unfamiliar: *super* (usually a red label on the pump) is a leaded substitute with an additive, it is very unlikely you will require this unless you are driving an older petrol engine vehicle; *sem chumbo* 95 and 98 (usually green or white labelling on the pump) are the lead-free grades; *gasoleo* (black labelling on the pump) is diesel. Diesel fuel is significantly cheaper than petrol, so if you are going to be doing a lot of driving and are hiring, bear this in mind.

Drive carefully, as the road is regarded as a pavement, especially in country areas. Be extra vigilant for animals and the ox-carts frequently encountered in country areas. Be aware also that roads, even main roads, almost invariably narrow appreciably where they cross bridges, and sometimes where they pass through small villages — and there are often *no warnings*. Conflicting or absent road signs and road markings can be disconcerting at times, so take extra care (a stop sign may not necessarily be accompanied by a white line on the road, for example). There are also some confusing and overly intricate road intersections (largely an inheritance from the days when roundabouts were not used and, because no-one knew whether traffic from the right had priority, they simply clogged up!). Now that it is clear that traffic already on the roundabout has priority, roundabouts are being built everywhere and have become prime sites for local authorities to place ever more remarkable works of art. Do beware, however, that the roundabout still confuses some local drivers; it is not uncommon to see a driver turn clockwise round the island in order to take the left exit!

The general standard of driving lacks the discipline to which we are

Branda da Bordença, a deserted village below Adrão, is passed on Car tour 3. Walk 9 takes you through this delightful spot, also shown on page 111.

accustomed. Anticipation is in short supply, which can give rise to dangerous situations, and this is particularly true in overtaking. It appears to be obligatory to overtake anything in the way, whatever the road conditions. There are frequent **police checks**, so make sure you have the relevant documents relating to your vehicle, your driving licence, and your passport to hand. Remember to take a **pocket phrase book**, if only for the road signs — you won't find them in English.

Bear in mind that the alcohol limit (0.5mg/l) is lower than in the UK. If you are involved in an accident you will automatically be tested; penalties can be steep. Using a mobile phone while driving is also subject to on-the-spot fines if you get caught. It is also compulsory to carry a reflective safety waistcoat and triangle in all vehicles; check for these if hiring.

The **touring notes** are brief; they include little history or information readily available in tourist office leaflets. We concentrate instead on the 'logistics' of touring: times and distances, road conditions, viewpoints and good places to rest or **picnic**. Most of all we emphasise possibilities for **walking**. While some of the walks may not be suitable during a long car tour, you may see a landscape that you would like to explore at leisure another day. Distances quoted in the text are *cumulative kilometres* from Viana or Ponte da Barca.

The touring map inside the back cover is designed to be held out opposite the touring notes and contains all the information you need to follow the notes. **Plans** of Ponte de Lima, Viana do Castelo, Ponte da Barca, Arcos de Valdevez and Braga are on pages 128-133; a plan of the Ribeira district of Porto is on pages 48-49. **A key to the symbols** in the notes is in the touring map legend. Allow plenty of time for **stops**: the shown times include only short breaks at viewpoints labelled (☞) in the touring notes.

Driving on **Sundays** can be particularly frustrating; it seems everyone turns out and no one knows quite where they are going. Sunday afternoon drivers were probably invented here! You will be much better off doing the car tours during the week (taking note of market days, which always cause local congestion).

If you have time for only one tour during your visit, don't miss Car tour 3, the Peneda-Gerês circuit.

All motorists should read the country code on page 14 and go quietly in the countryside.

Food, wine and markets

The traditional cuisine of the Minho is based very firmly on locally grown produce. While for many local people during much of the last century this meant a diet high in starch, with large portions of potatoes, maize bread and rice (in fact the Minhotos at that time had the highest carbohydrate intake of any Europeans, even beating Bulgaria), their diet today is far

Every village and town in the Minho has its own festa. The annual homage to the local saint provides the religious component which increasingly these days is overtaken by the more secular eating, drinking and dancing entertainment. Whatever, you will always find the locals ready to dress up in their vivid traditional dress.

better balanced, while retaining many of the traditional flavours and recipes.

Almost every household in the rural areas of the Minho will have its own vegetable patch, probably have a pig, *barrosā* calves and chickens, and produce much of its own food. This traditional fare translates itself onto the menu of most of the local restaurants, usually in portions that would go a long way to satisfying even the appetite of a hungry farmer at the end of a day's work.

One of the only 'external' components of the traditional Minho diet is — as everywhere else in Portugal — *bacalhau*, or dried cod. Today, however, you will find most restaurants offering a good selection of excellent fresh fish and seafood alongside the more traditional *bacalhau* and meat dishes. Eating out in Portugal is still very much a family occasion, often in the evenings, but especially weekends and Sunday lunchtimes. Eating times are much closer to English habits than Spanish,

The ubiquitous bacalhau, *served here with baked potatoes, olives,* broa *and red* vinho verde. *Wine is traditionally drunk from a bowl* (malga) *as shown here.*

with lunch from midday and dinner from 7.30pm.

A typical meal will start with some *entradas;* usually these appear on the table without being requested and can comprise — in addition to bread (often *broa* or maize bread) — smoked ham (*presunto*), olives (*azeitonas*), local cheese (*queijo*) and prawns (*camarãos*).

If you don't order soup at the start of your meal you can always, like many locals, have it at the end. In any case, if you don't have soup, especially the delicious vegetable soups, you may well begin to wonder what happens to all the vegetables you see growing, because traditionally not very much vegetable will appear with a main course. So be sure to try the *sopa de legumes* or the even more typical *caldo verde*, a shredded cabbage and potato soup with a slice of spicy sausage in it.

Main courses fall into the two categories of fish (*peixe*) or meat (*carne*). Excellent fresh fish is widely available. Look for the fish of the day (portions are often charged by weight); bass (*robalo*), turbot (*cherne*) hake (*pescada*) and sole (*linguado*) are fairly common. More specific to the Minho is the seasonal shad (*sável*) and, if you want to go really native

A free-range pig enjoying life (top); pork features widely in Minho recipes. Every household in rural Minho has its own colourful vegetable patch (middle and top right). Baked in a traditional oven (above), maize bread (broa) is a lovely crusty loaf.

(and have the money!), there is lamprey *(lampreia)* to be tried in the early months of the year. Sardines *(sardinhas)*, particularly tasty in late spring to early summer, are usually grilled with green peppers and onions and then served with boiled potatoes. Fresh fish will normally be grilled or fried, although you can have boiled hake with everything *(pescada cozida com todo)*, which will include potato, boiled cabbage and a boiled egg. There is no doubt though that king cod reigns supreme in the form of the ubiquitous bacalhau. There is said to be a different recipe for each day of the year (some even claim that over 1,000 recipes exist!). In rural areas it is still something of a 'special occasion' food and is traditionally served on Christmas eve.

Meat courses will normally be based on veal *(vitela)*, pork *(porco)*, goat *(cabrito)* or chicken *(frango)*. Peculiar to the Minho is the excellent meat from the *barrosã* cattle (see pages 70-71), producing a wonderfully flavoursome steak (try *posta mirandesa* to experience the flavour at its best). Veal and pork will usually be served in the form of chops *(costeletas)* or fillet *(febras)*. A wonderfully tasty way to have pork is in the form of *rojões*, a plate piled with marinated chunks, together with pork sausages, black pudding, and other pig parts — all served with roast potatoes and chestnuts. Usually there is so much that you can easily leave the parts which have less appeal to the English palate and still have a good fill. Roast goat *(cabrito assado)*, especially in the mountainous interior, can be exceptional, with its wonderfully rich flavour and usually very tender meat.

Desserts *(sobremesas)* are often a dieter's downfall. Full of eggs and sugar, they should only be considered as a reward for a long day's walking. Crème caramel *(pudim)*, crème brulée *(leite queimada)*, chocolate mousse *(mousse de chocolate)* are on most menus. Traditional in the Minho is *rabanadas,* a sweet fried bread with cinnamon and red wine sauce. But usually restaurants have fresh fruit as well.

Normally a meal will finish with coffee, and for the locals this will be the strong, black and richly aromatic drink which forms an essential part of daily life from breakfast to the end of dinner. If you find the black coffee too strong, try asking for a *meia de leite* (half coffee, half milk) or *galão* (half coffee, half milk diluted with water).

Of course, no meal in Portugal would be complete without wine. The Minho produces the well known *vinho verde* ('green' or young wine) which can be either red or white. To most foreign palates the white version is far more acceptable. Look out particularly for Muralhas de Monção and some of the Alvarinhos from Melgaço.

A little further south and from the neighbouring Douro Valley come some excellent *maduro* (mature) red wines as well, of course, as the internationally known port wines.

Left: treading the grapes; below: the river Douro upstream near Pinhão (see Wine tour, pages 46-49)

Market day at Ponte da Barca where, in addition to the usual fruit and veg, you can pick up live chickens, tableware or bacalhau *(second from bottom) — as well as some roasted chestnuts to munch while you shop.*

For local colour, hustle and bustle, and for an atmosphere of barely-restrained excitement, visit a local market. But be warned, some of them (like the one at Barcelos) are so large, that you are likely to spend the whole day there. The range of products on sale is mind-boggling. Whether you are looking for clothing or linen, or just new wooden wheels for your ox-cart, you'll find what you want. Markets are normally held either weekly or fortnightly; in a few cases they are monthly.

Weekly
Viana do Castelo: Fridays
Barcelos: Thursdays

Fortnightly
Ponte de Lima: Mondays
Ponte da Barca: Wednesdays
   (same week as Ponte de Lima)
Arcos de Valdevez: Wednesdays
   (alternate week to Ponte de
   Lima)
Vila Verde: Saturdays (alternates
   with Pico Regalados)

Monthly
Soajo: first Sunday of the month

Car tour 1: THE *VINHO VERDE* CIRCUIT

Viana do Castelo • Ponte de Lima • Ponte da Barca • Arcos de Valdevez • Melgaço • Sistelo • Arcos de Valdevez • Ponte de Lima • Viana do Castelo

234km/145mi; about 4h50min driving. This is a long day if you do the whole tour from Viana. Starting from Ponte de Lima cuts out about 50km. The route from Viana to Arcos and back can be frustrating driving on Sundays and peak holiday times (July and August).

On route: Picnics (see pages 10-13): (1), 3-8; Walks: (1, 2), 11

The winding nature of the roads either side of the Lima River and over to the Minho Valley makes for slow driving, but the road surfaces are good. In spring especially, heightened farming activity brings out the ambling ox-carts. These carts can create a major hazard when they pull out into the road or are hidden by a bend, so extra vigilance is always necessary.

Follow the river Lima upstream as it languidly flows through some of the loveliest countryside in Portugal, where the vines for the *vinho verde* are grown. It is easy to see why the Romans regarded the Lima as the 'River of Forgetfulness', making anyone who crossed it forget their native country and friends. Ponte de Lima boasted a fine Roman bridge, a short section of which remains on the northern bank, but the changing course of the river, due to silting, caused it to be extended in the 14th century. En route to Ponte da Barca and its 15th-century bridge, visit the interesting 11th-century Romanesque church at Bravães. Once across the bridge at Ponte da Barca, you leave the river Lima behind for the photogenic bridge spanning the river Vez at Arcos de Valdevez. These two rivers are slow-flowing and clear, so take your swimming things. You then pass over to the Minho Valley, visiting picturesque Melgaço and returning via the terraced hills of Sistelo.

Leave **Viana★** (*i✝⛽🏨🛏️✕⛺📮➕🌐🅿Ⓜ*WC; town plan pages 130-131) by taking the IC1 dual carriageway towards PORTO, crossing the river by the new bridge. Then take the first exit (4km) signposted to PONTE DE LIMA and PONTE DA BARCA, to follow the N203. This next section of road is fairly straight, passing through an area of mixed cultivation, houses and vineyards. Once past the paper mill on the right (11.2km) and the left turn to

Lanheses (14.5km), the scenery becomes more interesting, with hanging hayricks, impressive granite gateways, and granite posts holding up vines. Hidden valleys of the imposing granite mountain on the left, the **Serra de Arga**, feature in Walks 1 and 2. At **Vitorino das Donas** pass the road down left (18.2km) signposted 'Cais do Rio Lima', which leads quickly to the setting for Picnic 4, shown on pages 12-13.

Viana do Castelo — the main square and fountain, seen from the archway of the old town hall. Right: engraving above the church doorway at Bravães

Continuing ahead, reach an underpass and roundabout on the outskirts of **Ponte de Lima★** (*i✚🏛️✕🏤⊕M🚂📻* WC; town plan page 128). Unless it is market day* (alternate Mondays), drive straight through the underpass and in about 0.5km turn left towards the river down Largo Dr António Megalhães. Then bear right towards the old bridge shown overleaf, along

---

*If it is market day, turn right here, then left at the next roundabout in 0.9km, onto the Ponte de Lima bypass. Then turn left at another roundabout in a further 1.5km to Ponte de Lima centre — noting that a right turn at the same point leads up to Santa Madalena (Picnic 6; 🛆). Park either side of the dual carriageway. Return to the bypass and turn left to continue to Ponte da Barca.

Passeio 25 de Abril. There is parking by the road before the bridge and down to the left just beyond it (Picnic 5; 🛆), *but not on market days.*
Leave Ponte de Lima by continuing through the town along Rua do Rosário and Rua do São João, towards PONTE DA BARCA. Turn left on meeting the bypass road (27.2km).
Now you begin a most beautiful section of the tour, in the **Lima Valley**. Spreading vine tendrils form lovely arches and create a vibrant green

25

mantle over the countryside in spring. Shafts of sun, lighting up the hillsides, complete the enthralling pastoral vision. Reach **Bravães** (39.3km ♨); its 11th-century Romanesque church lies a further 0.5km along, on the left.

Continue to **Ponte da Barca★** (42.3km *i*♨🏠✕🚐⊕🏕🎦WC; town plan pages 128-129). At the first roundabout go straight ahead and, on reaching the T-junction in the old town, turn left (N101). The car park (43.5km) is now straight ahead

across the main road, which then goes round to the right to cross the old bridge (Picnic 7; photograph pages 32-33). Leave Ponte da Barca by turning left from the car park, to cross the old bridge and head towards ARCOS DE VALDEVEZ. Watch the traffic lights! Just 300m after crossing the bridge, look for a turning right with a blue signpost to the ESTAÇÃO VITIVINICOLA

Left: terraces at Avelar, seen on leaving the village during Walk 11. Below: Ponte de Lima is a very attractive market town with a lovely old square opening out onto the south side of the medieval bridge. If you take a look at the old keep house just downstream from the bridge (setting for Picnic 5) you will find the markings for flood levels — a remarkable testimony to the bridge builders' craft that their work has survived such tests over the centuries.

(there is also a brown ROTA VINHO VERDE sign). You may care to make a short (0.7km) detour to visit this establishment, which gives technical support to the whole *vinho verde* area.

Afterwards, return to the N101 to continue towards Arcos de Valdevez, passing under the new IC28 road to Ponte de Lima after about 1km.

At **Arcos de Valdevez**★ (47.5km *i*♦♠✕⊖⊕M⊓WC; town plan page 129) turn left at the first roundabout to cross the river, then turn right just after the bridge; there is parking by the river (limited on market days). Here you can stroll upstream alongside the river with pleasant views across to the old bridge near the town centre (Picnic 8; photograph pages 36-37). Continue the tour by following the N101 as it winds up, out of the Lima Valley, to the pass at **Portela** (66km). You now drop down into the **Minho Valley**, with beautiful views to the north across to Spain. Soon you are in an area of very extensive viniculture; much of the planting is now across the fields rather than just around the perimeter. This facilitates harvesting and spraying, but is also a reflection of the increased importance of viniculture and the decline of arable farming — a strange reversal of what happened when maize was introduced (see 'Agriculture and landscape, pages 69-73). After 80km you will pass the Brejoeira estate on the left; pause to look through the gates at the beautiful house and gardens. Turn right at the traffic lights (83km) on the

N202 towards Melgaço; you are now heading into the Alvarinho *vinho verde* sub-region.

To the left you will get glimpses of the Minho River and Spain beyond it. When you come to traffic lights at **Melgaço ★** (106km 🏨 ▲▲ ✕ 🏤 **M** 🍴WC), turn left and drive into the town centre, bearing left and left again (in front of the Banco Espirito Santo). You will come to a small tree-lined square with parking. It is well worth walking up into the old centre; you will find the Solar Alvarinho de Melgaço just along from the tower at the top of the town. Here you can sample up to six Alvarinhos free of charge! There is a display and museum explaining the whole process, and brochures from the local estates which can be visited. A good selection of wines is also on sale.

Now you should return on the N202 towards MONÇÃO (possibly visiting one of the estates on the way), taking care at 125.5km to look for the turning to MERUFE and SISTELO. Turn left on the N304 and follow signs for MERUFE and SISTELO. In 130.5km, where the road forks, keep right uphill. There are panoramic views along this high level road, which leads through woodland and old villages. **Merufe** (138km) is an elongated village spread alongside the road.

As the mountains become more rolling and the terrain less harsh, begin the descent towards Sistelo, across the valley to the right. Cross the bridge at the head of the **Rio Vez** (146km), from where there is a fine view down towards Arcos. Beyond the bridge, Sistelo is seen perched on a ridge, surrounded by amazingly steep terraced slopes.

Pass through **Sistelo** (149km); the views along the next stretch are especially fine. At **Cabreiro** (153km) note the left turn (156.5km) to Vilar and Avelar (Walk 11). Take care at the junction left to Mézio (169km); the right of way is uncertain.

Continue back into **Arcos** (172km) and then, at the roundabout by the new bridge, join the N202 back towards VIANA along the north side of the river Lima. Follow signs back to **Viana** (234km).

(An alternative to the N202 is to take the new IC28 back to Ponte de Lima. Join this by *crossing* the new bridge at the roundabout as you leave Arcos. Turn right at the next roundabout just after the bridge and head back towards Ponte da Barca, to join the IC28 after 2km. At Ponte de Lima you have to rejoin the N202 to Viana, but a new road, the IP9, is due to open on this stretch in 2005.)

Car tour 2: HISTORICAL PURSUITS

Ponte da Barca • Darque • Barcelos • Braga • Bom Jesus • Citânia de Briteiros • Guimarães • Ponte da Barca

190km/118mi; about 4 hours driving. Start from the bridge in Ponte da Barca, heading towards Viana on the N203.

On route: Picnics (see pages 10-13): (5, 6), 9; Walks 3-10 are within easy reach of Ponte da Barca.

An early start is needed for this very full day. Avoid Thursdays (market day in Barcelos, which merits a day out in itself), or bypass Barcelos and go directly to Braga. There is so much to see on this trip that spreading it over two days, with an overnight stop en route, would allow more time for sightseeing. On the whole the road surfaces are good. Beyond Bom Jesus, where more country roads are encountered, the surfaces become variable. Be alert for the occasional pothole and short bumpy stretch. If you are based in Viana, join the tour at the 39.5km-point (Darque).

A wealth of interest is captured in this tour, which visits Barcelos, home of the Barcelos cockerel legend (see page 31) and one of the largest weekly markets in Portugal; Braga, the religious capital, and nearby Bom Jesus, centre of

Baroque staircase at Bom Jesus (Picnic 9)

pilgrimage, renowned for its splendid baroque staircase; Citânia de Briteiros, the largest fortified Celto-Iberian hill settlement in Portugal; and Guimarães, the first capital of the Portuguese nation.

From the bridge at **Ponte da Barca★** (*i✝🛏️✕🏠⊕ ♫🏠WC; Picnic 7; town plan pages 128-129) follow the N203 towards VIANA. At **Ponte de Lima★** (*i✝🛏️✕🏠⊕M🏠🏠 WC; Picnics 5, 6; town plan page 128) keep on the bypass, to skirt the town (which is on your right). Turn right at the roundabout with the Braga road, then left at the roundabout/underpass (18.9km).

Ignore the turning onto the new IC1 at 38km but, at **Darque** (39.5km ✕🏠), turn left towards PORTO on meeting the old N13. At the roundabout (44.8km) carry straight on towards BARCELOS on the N103. Keep ahead at a major junction (52km). This is a pleasant run through a mixture of farmland and forest, with ample opportunities to pull off the road. A kilometre after passing a large statue of the Barcelos cockerel on the left (56.4km), there is a parking and picnic area under the trees on the right (🏠). Keep ahead at a roundabout (59.1 km), ignoring the sign left to Barcelos. Barcelos appears ahead — an 'island' in the middle of a farming community. Pass the slip road off right to Braga (but turn here if you are bypassing Barcelos). The road now circles to the right, under a bridge, to pass under itself and join another major road at the bottom. Reach a large roundabout with a huge fountain (64.2km), where BARCELOS is signposted straight on — but the exit road is nearly three-quarters of the way round.

Take the next right filter (65.8km; just before an underpass) into **Barcelos★** (*i✝🛏️✕△🏠⊕MWC). Keep ahead at the first roundabout and turn in right at the second, then continue ahead until you reach a huge open area on the left (67km) — the car park (except on Thursdays, when the market is held there). The tourist office ('Turismo') is situated in the prominent square tower.

Leave Barcelos by following the signs to BRAGA, passing the Turismo tower and soon heading round and down to the left, to a large roundabout decorated with pyramids; then cross the new bridge over the river. At the time of writing there were major road works in progress at the far side of the bridge, so *carefully* follow signs to BRAGA. (If there are no signposts for Braga, look for signs to BARCELINHOS.) You should emerge at a T-junction with a major dual carriageway (70.5km). Turn left here and take a further left turn at the next roundabout, to join the N103 to BRAGA (72km).

The road now leads through hamlets and farmland and passes the turning to the Porto motorway (80.2km). Just after driving under a major road, you reach a roundabout (85.1km). Go straight ahead in the direction of BRAGA OESTE, then keep ahead towards CENTRO (86.7km). At a busy roundabout (87km) again keep ahead, along a street (Rua

The Barcelos cockerel

Depending who you ask, or what book you read, you will get one of many versions of the legendary tale of the Barcelos cockerel. Whatever version you hear or read, there is no disputing the prominence that the story has locally and even nationally. Everywhere you go in Portugal you will see T-shirts, tea towels, coffee mugs, key rings and even mobile phones featuring the bright colours of this famous fowl.

All versions of the story have some common threads: there was a foreign pilgrim travelling northwards, through Portugal, towards Santiago de Compostela; he was arrested and charged with theft (or, in extreme versions of the tale, murder), found guilty and sentenced to death; after consistently protesting his innocence he finally sought recourse to St James himself and, in front of the judge (who was tucking into his dinner), he challenged that, if he was innocent, the cockerel on the platter in front of the judge, would stand up and crow. The rooster promptly obliged and the traveller was duly set free to continue northwards on his pilgrimage.

Ever since, the rooster has been a symbol of justice in the north of the country, and indeed has almost become a national emblem. So if you go to any market in the Minho — and especially Barcelos — you will find row upon row of brightly painted cockerels of all shapes and sizes made from the local potters' clay. No Minho home can be without one, and they do make delightful souvenirs.

Comendador Santos da Cunha) which has some arches at the far end. You should be able to find parking near these arches, which are just outside the old city walls of **Braga★** (88km *i✝🏔️✖🚉⊕* Mwc; town plan pages 132-133). Then walk up the road, alongside the wall on your right, into the square (Largo Paulo Orósio). Cross the square diagonally to the right, then go left, and then right to the centre.

Continue on towards Bom Jesus by heading straight downhill from the arches to the main road (N103), a dual carriageway. Turn right initially, back to a large roundabout with a statue and underpass. Avoid the underpass and go round left, around the roundabout (signposted for CHAVES and GUIMARÃES), to head back down the dual carriageway in the opposite direction. BOM JESUS (brown signs) and CHAVES are the signs to follow, as this dual carriageway takes you through two underpasses and then to a flyover (from which you get a first glimpse of Bom Jesus up to the right).

After the flyover, as you leave the Chaves road at a round-about, watch for the turn-off right signposted to BOM JESUS. At around 93.5km, as the road starts to wind up through the trees, there is a sign to the left for BELA VISTA. (A turn left here leads to a large parking and picnic area on the left — Picnic 9; and, further along on the right, the start of the walking route up to Bom Jesus. Immediately after, also on the right, is another large parking area for the *elevador* ride to the top.) If you are driving to the top, continue ahead, turning right off the main route to park. From **Bom Jesus**★ (95.6km ♦♠✕⚠☎WC) there is a wonderful panorama over Braga.

To reach Citânia de Briteiros, which isn't signposted at this point, turn right on leaving Bom Jesus, to continue up the hill. Keep left at the fork (96km; signposted for CITÂNIA and GUIMARÃES), to enjoy a pleasant run along an elevated road through woodland. As the road descends, swing left towards CITÂNIA (100km), which can be seen on the hill ahead. There are fantastic views on both sides of the road; you pass through **Sobreposta** before reaching **Citânia de Briteiros**★ (105.3km ☎⚠☎). Park on the left and walk up the cobbled track opposite the car park, to the forestry house which is the entrance to the site. It is easy to appreciate the magnificent position of this Celto-Iberian hill settlement, which provides an excellent viewpoint over the surrounding countryside. Guimarães is reached by continuing in the same direction when you leave Citânia. Turn left at the junction at 107.4km (signposted to GUIMARÃES), then, in **Briteiros**, go right at the next junction (108.8km; signposted to GUIMARÃES and

TAIPAS). Notice the vines growing up the trees in this area. Pass through **Barco** and, at **Taipas** (113.5km ✕🍴), which has a market on Mondays, turn left towards GUIMARÃES on meeting the main road (N101).

At **Guimarães★** (117.7km *i*🛉 🎥🏰✕⛺🍴⊕Mwc) keep ahead, under a road bridge. Then, at the roundabout in front of the Bombeiros (fire station), keep ahead and slightly right. Park on the right just after this roundabout (120.3km) and then walk straight on to the centre.

Leave Guimarães by circling to the right, following the sign to ESTÁDIO (stadium) and turning right again at the next roundabout (with two standing figures). Continue ahead, with the stadium on your right, then bear right at the next junction and immediately left, to rejoin the road by which you entered. Following signs for BRAGA will

take you back to the N101 (121.1km). Turn up right, away from the Braga road, into **Taipas** (127km ✕🍴) and turn right in the centre towards PÓVOA DE LANHOSO. Ignore the left turn to 'Citânia' at **Briteiros** (131.7km); keep ahead.

As you pass through **Vilela** (137.1km) the castle at Lanhoso is ahead on a hill. At a roundabout (with standing stones; 140.5km) turn left — just before the centre of **Póvoa de Lanhoso** (🎥✕⛺🍴). Follow the signs towards GERÊS and BRAGA by turning left at the next roundabout. Head uphill out of Lanhoso, with the castle now to the right (142.3km). Take a right turn to GERÊS in 143.2km, and then a left turn to AMARES some 500m further on. Go through **Monsul** (147.5km) and turn right to AMARES at the major junction (152.3km), immediately crossing the **Rio Cavado** on a new bridge (you get a good view of the fine old bridge off to the right). Once across the bridge, keep round to the left at the first roundabout, following the sign to AMARES POENTE. At the next roundabout (153.8km) turn left, following signposting to VILA VERDE — where the centre of **Amares** (🏰✕🍴wc) is straight ahead. At the next roundabout (155.7km) keep ahead on the BRAGA road. You arrive at **Rendufe** (159.1 km),

Ponte da Barca (Picnic 7) has a fine medieval bridge, alongside which is a small covered market. Before the bridge was built this was an important ferry crossing point, and the old buildings on the south side of the bridge formed the original part of the town.

where you should take the right turn, signposted to *RENDUFE MOSTEIRO* (monastery). You pass the monastery (160.5km ♠) where the road swings left, and continue on to the bridge at **Loureira**. Beyond the bridge bear right uphill; then, at the roundabout (163.2km) go straight ahead to **Vila Verde** (167km ✕🏪⊕WC). Turn right in the centre, on the main N101 to *PONTE DA BARCA* and *MONÇÃO*. Fruit sellers line the road at around 174km, and there are spectacular views and a viewpoint on the right in 177.2km (📷), with another viewpoint on the left 3km further on.

You enter **Ponte da Barca** after 187.8km, and come to the bridge in a further 2.2km. Now those based at Viana should follow the first part of the touring notes as far as Darque, then turn right.

Left: the emerald-green setting of a watermill some 1h48min along the route of Walk 3; the walk starts at São Miguel, 14km from Ponte da Barca. Below: the river Lima just above Ponte da Barca. This is probably one of the most peaceful stretches of the river, before reaching the Touvedo Reservoir and more rugged scenery beyond.

Car tour 3: PENEDA-GERÊS NATIONAL PARK AND SIERRA DE XURÉS NATURAL PARK

Ponte da Barca • Arcos de Valdevez • Nossa Senhora da Peneda • Castro Laboreiro • Entrimo • Lindoso (or Lobios • Portela do Homem) • Germil (or Brufe) • Ponte da Barca

160km/100mi; about 4.5 hours driving. Start from the bridge at Ponte da Barca (town plan pages 128-129), heading for Arcos de Valdevez.

On route: Picnics (see pages 10-13): 2, 7, 8, 10, 11, 12; Walks: 5-10, 12

Those based at Viana can use the notes for Car tour 1 to link up with the start of this tour. Generally road conditions are good, but be aware that some sections are narrow and mountainous. This is particularly so on the Portela do Homem option, with one stretch in particular which should only be driven by experienced motorists. This option also involves some 5km of dirt road — of reasonable standard, but slow going.

Enjoy the wildness and splendour of this little-known corner of Portugal and the magnificent sanctuary of Nossa Senhora da Peneda situated beneath a towering granite mountain in the heart of the park. Wonder at the rugged setting of the castle at Castro Laboreiro, before continuing briefly into Spain and the Sierra de Xurés Natural Park. Here you pass through some really wild scenery before dropping down to the Lima Valley, where you can choose whether to continue round to Portela do Homem or carry straight on down the Lima Valley to Lindoso. In either case we then lead you up to a drive along the uplands separating the Lima and Homem valleys, with breathtaking views and good opportunities for bird watchers.

Start from the old bridge at **Ponte da Barca★** (*i*♁♠✕🅿⊕ 🅰🖼WC; Picnic 7), taking the N101 across the bridge, towards ARCOS DE VALDEVEZ. As you come to the first roundabout at **Arcos de Valdevez★** (3.7km; town plan page 129), turn right, following a brown sign to the PARQUE NACIONAL PENEDA GERÊS (PNPG). Quickly coming to a T-junction, turn right.* Almost immediately (4.3km), turn left, following a green sign to the park.

*A left turn at this point would take you over the old road bridge and into the centre of Arcos (*i*♁♠✕🅿⊕M🅰WC; Picnic 8).

35

Now on the N202, you shortly pass in front of a hill topped with the ruins of the medieval fortified manor house of **Paço de Giela** (⛪) and, at 6.3km, take the right turn signposted to AZERE, GRADE and MÉZIO. The road now climbs steadily up towards Mézio and the PNPG. At 15.4km you will find a small viewing area on the left hand side of the road (📷); it's worth stopping here to take in the views over terraced hillsides and ancient villages. You are looking across to the villages of Vilela and Bostelinhos (Walk 8), while up to the right you can see the high summits of Bicos (Walk 7).

Soon you reach the **Mézio** entrance to the PNPG (18km ⚲△🛱; Picnic 2). There are several well-preserved dolmen in the vicinity of the road junction. If you turn left here, after 300m you will come to a visitors' centre (***i***, but with

36

infrequent opening hours). Whether or not the centre is open, you might like to follow its short (2km) waymarked interpretation walk. Carrying on up this side road would take you to the starting points for Walks 7 and 8.

From Mézio the main tour carries on along the N202 towards SOAJO, passing an equestrian centre off to the left (19km 🐎). The road swings round and out of the pine woods to give extensive views off to the south, over the Lima Valley to the Serra Amarela, Ermida (Walk 4) and Germil (Walk 3). Note that the N202 mysteriously becomes the N304 at this point! At 20.6km you come to a left turn, signposted to Peneda. If you don't want to visit Soajo, you can take this left and rejoin the tour at the 28km-point below. After 24km you reach the outskirts of **Soajo** (⛺✕WC;

Arcos de Valdevez has a pleasant riverside front and old bridge (Picnic 8). The river Vez is said to be one of the cleanest rivers in Europe; this may explain why it harbours one of the most successful otter populations in Portugal.

market on the first Sunday of the month). Carry on down the main road to a large stone monument (25km). Turn left here and follow this road for 200m, to arrive at the *espigueiros* ★ of Soajo. This national monument is the starting point for Walk 9, while Walk 10 starts further down the same road. The *espigueiros* (photograph pages 108-109) are well worth visiting. They are in a group, situated on a rocky promontory just on the outskirts of the village. In the centre of the group is a large open space of bare rock — an *eira* (threshing floor), used for drying and threshing the maize.

After visiting the *espigueiros,* turn back along the same road and, on reaching the monument, turn right, back up the main road. Then turn right again immediately. This will

bring you into Soajo's lovely old village square, complete with its pillory (photographs on page 112).

Return to the main road and turn right, passing the Espigueiro Restaurant on your right. Just past here, as you go around a right-hand bend, take the steep cobbled road up to the right (signposted to GAVIEIRA). This narrow road climbs steeply out of Soajo. Soon (now on tarmac), you will pass some fine old *abrigos* as you drive up into a desolate, rocky landscape (see pages 40, 56 and 96). At 28km, at a junction with dirt tracks, the road swings away to the left and almost immediately rises to another tarmac road, where you have to turn sharp right uphill. *(This is the point where the route avoiding Soajo rejoins the main tour.)*

Two kilometres further on you pass a forestry house (the **Casa Abrigo**; 30km; Picnic 10). Shorter walk 9-1 begins here. Up ahead you can see the beginnings of Adrão; below in the valley lies the deserted village of Branda da Bordença, which is on the route of Walk 9 (photograph pages 16-17). Another 2km brings you to **Nossa Senhora da Paz** (32km ♟⌂). There is a small picnic area here under the trees (Picnic 12), and it is worth walking to the top of the hill with a cross on it (just beyond the church) to take in some splendid views down to Soajo

Continued on page 42

Peneda-Gerês National Park

The Peneda-Gerês National Park (PNPG) is Portugal's only protected area with this status. It was established in 1971, covering an area of approximately 70,000 hectares adjacent to the Spanish border. In 1997 a formal link with the Spanish 'Parque Natural Baixa Limia-Sierra de Xurés' was established, with the formation of the trans-frontier Gerês-Xurés park. Cross border co-ordination and collaboration has subsequently brought significant benefits in the protection and re-establishment of various species.

The park can be split into three regions: the southeast, where the Serra do Gerês reaches up

Trapela (Walk 10) lies below the Serra do Soajo, in the northern reaches of the Peneda-Gerês National Park

to 1538m; the centre, where the Serra Amarela (photograph overleaf) rises to 1369m; and the north, where the Serra do Soajo and Serra da Peneda attain 1416m.

By far the most widespread rock type in the park is granite, although in the extreme north there are schists and in the centre some quartzites and meta-sediments.

Both the eagle owl (Bubo bubo; top left) and the golden eagle (Aquila chrysaetos; top right) are present in the national park, where you'll also see some remarkably formed granite outcrops (bottom).

There are various types of granite which have influenced the landscape. The oldest granites, which have suffered greater alteration and breakdown of the feldspar component, form the softer, more rounded topography of the Serra Amarela, Serra do Soajo and Castro Laboreiro plateau, while younger granites form the more rugged uplands of the Serra da Peneda and Serra do Gerês. The whole of the upland landscape has been subjected to glacial and periglacial conditions.

The eastern part of the park is less accessible and much of the upland is extensive bare rock. We tend to concentrate on the central and northern parts, where access is simpler, where there is more contrast in smaller areas, and where there

has been more agricultural activity to create added interest. We also deliberately avoid the area around Caldas do Gerês itself, as this gets far too crowded at weekends and in the summer.

Being located between Mediterranean and north European bio-systems, with terrain lying between 200m and 1500m, and with everything from bare rock to rich, lush pastures and deep woodland, it is hardly surprising that the PNPG offers interest at every turn to the botanist. What you see will depends very much on the time of year, but perhaps the most rewarding time is from late April to mid-June.

The fauna within the park area, and particularly the larger

This village of abrigos, Branda de Cobernos, lies on the route of Walk 7. The buildings blend perfectly into the bare granite landscape.

The Iberian wolf *Canis lupus* is holding its own, the roe deer *Capreolus capreolus* (symbol of the park) is now the subject of a renewed conservation programme, and the wild goat is increasing in numbers. The park has a significant otter population, due to the largely unpolluted watercourses. Bird life, particularly among the larger raptors, is also recovering, with buzzard *Buteo buteo*, peregrine *Falco peregrinus*, kestrel *Falco tinnunculus*, merlin *Falco columbarius*, hobby *Falco subbuteo*, Montagu's harrier *Circus pygargus*, and even golden eagle *Aquila chrysaetos* present in increasing numbers.

Man's early occupation in the area is well evidenced, with some of the largest concentrations of dolmen in the Iberian Peninsula to be found near Castro Laboreiro. Other groups are found at Mézio and in the Serra Amarela. Iron Age fortifications are present at Parada, Ermida and Tourém.

species, have suffered considerably since the park was formed, largely due to the conflicting interests of the local inhabitants, indiscriminate hunting and the destruction of habitats through forest and heath fires. Things are improving, however, and it appears that the decline has been reversed — helped considerably by the cross-border collaboration already referred to.

This sea of yellow gorse, seen at the 1h40min-point in Walk 8, could partly explain the name of the adjacent Serra Amarela ('yellow mountains').

Right: If you're walking in the park in summer, you may wonder why the stone slab bridges are necessary, as the streams are frequently dry. But after winter rains the picture is very different! This bridge is crossed at the 2h23min-point on Walk 3, near Germil.

Below: threshing with a traditional malhoa; *maize drying; splendidly yoked oxen, carting broom and bracken for cattle bedding (seen above Avelar on Walk 11)*

There is significant evidence of the Roman presence, particularly the road from Braga to Astorga (the Portela do Homem optional return for Car tour 3 follows this route beside the Vilarinho Reservoir). Middle Age remains include the monasteries at Ermelo and Pitões das Júnias, together with the castles of Castro Laboreiro and Lindoso. There are even some abandoned medieval villages. Over the last decade, road-building has made much of the park more accessible. Even so, the continuing rural depopulation (with especially the younger people abandoning the tenuous livelihood to be won from these remote hills and fields) has resulted in much of the communal structure and traditional way of working vanishing. But it is still to be found in isolated pockets, and you will certainly come across it as you follow some of the walks we describe.

41

Ploughing with oxen near Peneda

and the Lima Valley.
Passing above the village of **Adrão**, the road takes you round the valley, past another forestry house on the right. At 35.5km, turn up left uphill, following the sign to PENEDA. You climb over a pass and emerge at a viewpoint on the right (37km 🎦). Pause here to take in the stunning view ahead of you; huge bare granite slopes, deep, deep valleys with villages far below, and — far in the distance — your first glimpse of the sanctuary at Peneda, lost in this huge landscape.

The road now drops steeply, past the small hamlet of **Tibo** and on down towards Rouças, where terraced fields provide a welcome contrast to the awesome slopes above. Pass through **Rouças**, forking downhill to the right as you leave the village (41km), and gaining some attractive views back to the fields below the village from the other side of the valley. You now pass round into the Peneda Valley proper and, at 46km*, as you cross a

bridge, you begin to see the huge granite backdrop to the sanctuary (see photograph on page 124). Turn left at a T-junction (48km), to park at **Nossa Senhora da Peneda** (🚻WC), where Walk 12 begins and ends.

After your visit, return to the junction and continue straight ahead towards LAMAS DE MOURO The road follows the valley up to a pass (53km), topped with a small shrine on the left, then drops quickly down into the valley beyond, through more mixed woodland. All along this stretch you can see traces of the old Cistercian monks' way from Ermelo (south of Soajo) to Fiães (near Melgaço). You pass the PNPG interpretation centre and campsite (**Merindos**; 56km *i*△🛒; Picnic 11). Just 500m further on, turn right and immediately right again at **Lamas de Mouro** (✕△🛒🏕). The scenery becomes softer now, as you head towards CASTRO LABOREIRO. The oak trees are festooned with moss and lichen

---

*If you park by the bridge and follow the track upstream alongside the river, this quickly

becomes a granite trail which leads up to the sanctuary — a lovely short walk of just 1km.

— a sign of just how humid the climate is in these hills. This countryside has an ancient feel to it and, in fact, just to the north and east of Castro Laboreiro lies probably the greatest concentration of megalithic monuments and remains to be found in the Iberian Peninsula.

The road leads up to a traffic island and viewpoint (65km ☞) at the far end of **Castro Laboreiro** (🛏🏔✕△). It's worth stopping to take in yet another fabulous view; this one including the castle perched on its impressive craggy outcrop. It's just a short walk over to this castle but, be warned, a vertiginous scramble is involved in reaching the top! The road continues past the Restaurant Miradouro Castelo, passing the old church and leaving the village over a bridge (note the old bridge and watermill here, down to the right) in the direction of AMEIJOEIRA. Turn right (signposted to FRONTEIRA; 66.3km), and you will begin to pass through some really wild mountainous scenery. It's worth taking the short (0.5km) detour (signposted left at 68.2km) to **Ponte Cainheiras**, then continue down this wild valley, passing numerous little shrines *(alminhas)*; this was one of the pilgrimage routes to Santiago de Compostela. Take care to bear left (70.6km; *not signposted*), and you will come to the **frontier with Spain** (73km; note the old frontier marker post up on the right). Today, of course, the frontier is a non-event; but it is worth remembering that this has only been so for a very few years, and the circuit you are making would have been

impossible 15 years ago, when there was only one crossing point into Spain (at Melgaço). You are now entering the **Parque Natural Baixa Limia-Sierra de Xurés**, the natural extension of PNPG on the Spanish side of the border (see notes on page 38).

Continue down to **Entrimo** (82km ✝🏔✕), passing the fine church on the left and continuing along the main street, ignoring signs right to 'Portugal'. (For an excellent Galician meal, try Meson Beni in the village.) Take the right turn at the crossroads (86km). The road drops down towards the Lima River, affording some wonderful views out across the southern limb of the park. When you reach the main 540 road (95km), turn right (🍴 after 1km).

You cross the **Conchas Reservoir** and, just beyond (98km), come to a road junction where you have a choice: left to Portela do Homem or right to Lindoso. We describe both options (the routes rejoin above Germil), but you should consider the following before making your decision. The 'easy' route is to the right (Lindoso). The Portela do Homem option involves driving on a 5km stretch of dirt road; during weekends in the summer this section gets very busy and may, in July and August, be subject to a toll or even closure.

Lindoso option: Continue round to the right after crossing the bridge. You drive back into **Portugal** (107.5km) and come to the turning left (111km) for the castle at **Lindoso** (🛏✕M☞🍴). Turn in here; it's worth visiting the

castle museum (small entry
charge) and looking out over
the more than 60 *espigueiros*
grouped below the castle walls.
There is also a huge communal
oven in the castle confines.
Continue westwards along the
main road, passing the turning
to Soajo and dropping down
towards the smaller **Touvedo
Reservoir** (this was built to act
as a buffer to the main Lindoso
dam in order to maintain a
more regular flow downstream
in the Lima). At **São Miguel**
(also called Entre-Ambos-os-
Rios; 126km ✻△), take the
left turn (just before a bridge)
towards GERMIL and ERMIDA,
passing Café Novas Pontes (see
Walks 3 and 4) on the left.
Pass the cemetery on the left
and, just after a blue-painted
building on the right, turn
right by a stone cross (127km).
You have to drive a short way
on a very narrow road between
houses for 100m; then turn left
uphill after 200m and rise to a
T-junction with a tarmac road
(127.5km). Turn right here,

and keep on this road as it
leads you through a beautiful
valley all the way up to **Germil**
(136km). Pass through the
village and continue into ever-
higher open landscapes, with
rocks and tors punctuating the
heather- and bracken-covered
moorland.
In 139km you will come to a
T-junction. *This is where the
Portela do Homem option rejoins
from the left.* Turn right here (a
left turn would take you to
Brufe for Walks 5 and 6). You
rapidly drop down through the
isolated hamlet of **Bergaço**,
after which you need to turn
right (140.5km) towards STO
ANTÓNIO. You are now
travelling along the **watershed
between the Lima and
Homem valleys**. Enormous
vistas open out — initially to
the south and later to the
north. Take your time here; in
spring and early summer you
will almost certainly spot some
of the large raptors (buzzards,
golden eagle and Montagu's
harriers are all possibilities).
Bear right by a water tank
(143km) and soon emerge at
the back of the church in
Santo António (✻🅰WC). The
church could almost be
something out of Walt Disney,
with its twin circular turreted
towers. On the second Sunday
of June, farmers from miles
around bring their cattle here
for the annual blessing,
followed by a hearty open-air
lunch on the nearby hill slopes.
Continue due west, briefly over
a cobbled surface. You will
circle round to a stretch of road
offering particularly grand
views out over the north of the
park, all the way back to

Above: moss-covered steps at Lindoso Castle; right: this small shrine is in the wall of a house at Brufe, just at the start of Walk 6.

Peneda and Soajo. When you come down to a crossroads with a café on the right (148.5km), turn right.* Curve above **Azias** and follow this road downhill through **Sampriz**, to arrive back in **Ponte da Barca** (163km).

Portela do Homem option. Turn left at the junction past the bridge (98km) and you will shortly arrive in **Lobios** (🏨✕🅿). Turn right here; the road takes you gradually up into ever more mountainous scenery, until you arrive at **Portela do Homem** and re-enter **Portugal** (114km). From this pass you descend through some wonderful old oak forest, until you come to a dirt road turning downhill to the right (118km; signposted to VILARINHO/CAMPO GERÊS). Take this turn and you will come down alongside the **Vilarinho Reservoir** (note that you are not allowed to stop or park on this stretch of road — part of the old Roman route between Braga and Astorga). At a road junction (125km) you regain tarmac; turn right here to descend to the dam. (From the far side of the dam a short walk leads to the remains of the drowned village of Vilarinho.) Cross the dam and follow a very narrow, twisty mountain road; this leads you quite spectacularly up to **Brufe** (131km ✕🅿; Walks 5 and 6). Drive through the village, bearing left at the stone cross (132km) and taking the right turn shortly after passing the church. This road will take you past **Cutelo** (Walk 5; photographs pages 71, 87, 88), to a road junction (136km). Turn left here, and follow the notes for the Lindoso option from the 139km-point, to return to **Ponte da Barca** (160km).

---

*Or, if you wish to visit the wolf trap shown on page 92, turn left, and left again after another 1.4km. Then follow signs to FOJO DE LOBO, taking care not to miss the sharp right onto a dirt road at 3.5km. The trap is reached in another 200m along this dirt road.

Wine tour: PORTO AND THE RIVER DOURO

Viana do Castelo (or Braga) • Porto • Douro River trip

72km/45mi from Viana to Porto via the IC1; 1h15min driving; or 51km/32mi from Braga to Porto via the A3; 1h driving

While this tour could be done in a day, you will be hard pushed to do this and have a meaningful trip up the river. Far better to set aside at least two days, one for Porto itself (and the wine lodges) and the second for a full day on the Douro. Short river trips are on offer, but these do not reach the best scenery upstream. There are excellent hotels in Porto and along the banks of the river.

To visit Porto and take a cruise up the river Douro is a must, one of the highlights of a visit to northern Portugal. If possible, the best time to make this tour is in September, during the *vindima* — the time when the sun-ripened grapes for port wine are harvested and when production starts for the new season's wine.

Porto, the second city of Portugal, is far more closely linked geographically, historically and commercially to the hinterland of its river than is Lisbon to the Tagus. The Douro has shaped and influenced almost every aspect of the Porto's development since earliest times. Because of this, one of the best ways for the visitor to start getting to know Porto is from the river-front (Ribeira). This is also where you'll find various options to join boat tours upstream to complete the picture.

Traffic in and around **Porto** is chaotic, so we strongly recommend that you park on the outskirts and take a taxi down, for example, to the Palácio da Bolsa (which is just behind the river-front; see plan of Ribeira overleaf). Another option would be to park at the airport and take the 'Aerobus' into the city centre.

From the **Palácio da Bolsa** it is an easy walk down to Rua Infante D Henrique, where there is an INFORMATION CENTRE. Pick up a town plan and any other leaflets of interest. Then continue downhill, taking any one of the myriad of narrow streets and alleyways that lead down to the waterfront. Turn left here and wind your way along towards **Praça da Ribeira**.

Much of the Ribeira has under-gone extensive restoration as part of the Porto 2001 European Cultural Capital programme and has been declared a UNESCO World Heritage Site. You will quickly begin to soak in the history as you walk along; it surrounds you. Facing the river is a wonderful mix of old houses, tiny doorways, windows, bars and cafés.

Ahead is the double-decked **Dom Luis I Bridge** (the upper deck, now closed to traffic, will be used for the new metro), while across the river on the south bank, in Vila Nova de Gaia, you will see the Port wine lodges. All the famous names are represented — Calem, Taylor, Sandeman, Cockburn, Croft, and all of them will be delighted to show you around. You are free to

visit as many as you choose, depending on your capacity for port! It's an easy walk across the bridge but, be warned, to reach some of the wine lodges on the other side you will have a stiff uphill walk. It's worth the effort; you will get the best views of the Ribeira and at least the way back is all downhill…

(Port also features in one of the gastronomic specialities of the region, *morangos com porto*, strawberries with port wine — the perfect *sobremesa* following a good Portuguese meal.)

Several boat tour operators have booking offices in Praça da Ribeira. Take a look at the **Douro River trips** on offer while you are there and make your booking. As a general

Porto scenes: one of the many bridges over the Douro in the heart of the city (top); wine boats (barcos de rabelo) from the various port lodges on the river-front; colourful old buildings and alleyways; the tram line

47

rule, *the further up the river you go, the better*. There are many options, and to make it worthwhile, including visits to famous wineries and estates, you will need a full day at least. (Two-day and even week-long trips are also available.) Frequently the tours combine an upstream boat journey with a return by train (sometimes a steam train).

A typical day's boat tour would leave Ribeira (take care, some tours leave from the opposite quay at Vila Nova de Gaia, in front of the Port wine lodges) at 08.00. Following breakfast on board, you pass through the lock gates at **Crestuma**. Lunch, again served on board, would see you at the next lock gate, **Carrapatelo**. From here

on the scenery gets more and more interesting, as you pass **Regua** and the river reaches into the heart of the **demarcated Port wine area** (one of the oldest demarcated regions in the world, created in 1756). By mid-afternoon the boat will be passing the final lock-gates (at **Bagaúste**), before arriving at **Pinhão** at about 17.30. The return leg is usually by bus, with arrival back in Porto at about 20.00.

If you have the time, an overnight stay in Pinhão (▲✕) would allow you to travel further upriver by train the next day — to **Pocinho**, currently the end of the line (the remaining stretch to the Spanish frontier is closed, but the track is still in place and

*On the Douro River near Pinhão
(see also photograph page 22)*

there is talk of re-opening it for tourist traffic). The train journey would take you along the most spectacular part of the Douro Valley.

Then you could take the train all the way back to Porto — much more enjoyable than returning by coach. Trains depart from Pinhão to Pocinho at 10.35 and 17.32. In either case there is a short stop before the train returns to Pinhão and carries on to Regua, where there is a connection on to Porto. The train journey from Pocinho to Porto will take about four hours in all.

There are many variations to the trip outlined above, so it pays to shop around.

Useful contacts

Emergency: Tel 112
PNPG (National Park):
  Tel 253 203 480; www.icn.pt

Tourist offices
RTAM (Alto Minho Tourist Board): Tel 258 820 270; www.rtam.pt
Turismo (Ponte da Barca): Tel 258 452 899
Turismo (Viana do Castelo): Tel 258 822 620
Turismo (Ponte de Lima): Tel 258 942 335
Turismo (Terras de Bouro): Tel 253 391 133
Turismo (Arcos de Valdevez): Tel 258 510 260

Bus services
Auto Viação Cura: Tel 258 829 348
Auto Viação do Minho: Tel 258 800 340

Maps
IGEOE: Tel 218 505 300; www.igeoe.pt

Rural accommodation
ADERE: Tel 258 452 250; www.adere-pg.pt
Turihab (Turismo de Habitação): Tel 258 741 672; www.turihab.pt
Manor Houses Portugal; www.inn-portugal.com

Douro River trips
Rota Ouro: Tel 223 759 042; www.rotadouro.com
  Office and departures from **11**
Endouro: Tel 222 084 161; www.endouroturismo.pt
  Office and departures from **9**
Douro Azul: Tel 223 402 500; www.douroazul.com
  Office at **9** ; departures from **10**
Tomaz do Douro: Tel 222 082 286
  Office and departures from **9**

1 Tourist offices
2 Sé (Cathedral)
3 Palacio da Bolsa
4 Casa do Infante
5 San Francisco church
6 Torre dos Clérigos
7 Railway station
8 Santa Clara church
9 Ribeira quay
10 Vila Nova de Gaia quay
11 Serra do Pilar monastery
🚗 Car parking
⚱ Wine lodges
---- World Heritage Site boundary

Vila Nova de Gaia

❀ Walking

Northern Portugal offers fine opportunities for walking, especially in the magnificent Peneda-Gerês National Park (see pages 38-41). Shaped like a horseshoe, the national park lies against the eastern border with Spain. It includes several mountain ranges within its boundaries, but our walks are confined largely to the central Serra Amarela and the Serra da Peneda to the north. Here the huge granite mountains, rising to a height of 1416m (4650ft) at Pedrada, may at first appear barren and hostile, but they present a much kinder face when you walk amongst them. Rushing, tumbling streams, Romanesque bridges, old watermills, huge granite tors, soft green valleys, isolated villages, a host of wild flowers and interesting bird life are ingredients which combine to create visually stunning landscapes for you to discover.

When you are out and about in the mountains, please accept some words of caution. Distances in the mountains are very deceptive, and points that look close can sometimes take many hours of walking to bridge. Only do the walks described here (or established, waymarked walks created by the Park Authority), and never try to get from one walk to another via old trails shown on *any* maps, as they may no longer be viable (see 'maps' below).

There are walks in this book for everyone. All the walks are graded, so just check the grade to see if it suits you. If the grade of the main walk is too high, be sure to look over all the shorter versions. **If you are an inexperienced walker,** or just looking for a gentler walk, then go for the walks graded 'easy'. Look, too, at the picnic suggestions on pages 10-13; these particularly beautiful settings often present the opportunity for a short walk nearby. **Experienced walkers** should be able to tackle all of the walks in this book, taking into account, of course, the season and the weather conditions.

If a walk is very long, do be sure of your fitness before you attempt it. Don't tackle the more strenuous walks in high summer; do protect yourself from the sun, and carry an ample supply of water and plenty of fruit with you. **Always remember that storm damage or bulldozing could make some of the walks described in this book unsafe.** Always err on the side of safety; if you have not reached one of our landmarks after a reasonable time, then you must return to the last 'sure' point and start again.

Guides, waymarks, maps

Official **guides** are not available, but none is needed for the walks in this book. Most of the walks use well-established footpaths, trails and tracks, and are easily followed. With two exceptions (Walks 6 and 12), there is no official **waymarking**, but unofficial (and sometimes confusing) waymarks can sometimes be seen along parts of some of the walks. Where these are useful, we draw your attention to them. Otherwise, to avoid any possible confusion, *it is wiser to follow our directions at all times, in preference to any route markings.*

The **maps** in this book are the most useful you will find for guiding you through the walks. They are based on Portuguese government 1:25,000 military maps, but we have updated them on the terrain. If you want to see areas not shown on our maps, full sheets can be purchased from your local map stockist. Most of these maps are quite recent (based on surveys from 1995 onwards) but, even at this scale, it is not possible to include all the trails and minor tracks that exist. The maps are published by the Instituto Geográfico do Exército (www.igeoe.pt). The walking region covered by this book includes sheets 9, 14, 15, 16, 17, 27, 28, 29 and 30 of the M 888 series.

What to take

If you are already in Portugal when you find this book, and you haven't any special equipment such as a rucksack and walking boots, you can still do some of the walks — but better still, buy some of the equipment you need locally. Boots, shoes, and trainers can all be bought fairly cheaply, provided you do not require a large size. Continental size 45 is often the upper limit for men and 41 for women. Don't attempt any of the difficult walks without the proper gear, or with brand new footwear.

For each walk in the book, the minimum year-round equipment is listed. Where walking boots are required there is, unfortunately, no substitute: you will need to rely on the grip and ankle support they provide, and they are absolutely essential on some walks, where the path descends steeply over loose stones. All other walks should be made with stout shoes, preferably with thick rubber soles to grip on wet and slippery surfaces.

You may find the following checklist useful:

walking boots (which must be broken-in and comfortable)
spare bootlaces
waterproof rain gear (outside summer months)
long-sleeved shirt (for sun protection)
anorak (zip opening)
long trousers, tight at the ankles (sun and tick protection)
woollen hat and gloves
two fleeces
extra pair of (long) socks

sunglasses, sunhat, sun cream
first-aid kit, including plasters, bandages, antiseptic cream
insect repellent
water bottle with water purifying tablets
plastic plates, cups, etc
knives and openers
plastic groundsheet
compass, whistle, torch
small rucksack
compact folding umbrella
binoculars
mobile phone

Please bear in mind that there are significant seasonal variations in temperature and humidity; you should not underestimate just how hot or exposed some walks might be in high summer or how cold in winter. For this reason we have listed under 'Equipment' *all* the gear you might need, depending on the season, and we rely on your good judgement to modify it accordingly. Beware of the sun and the effects of dehydration. Don't be deceived by light cloud cover; you can still get sunburnt. It's tempting to wear shorts for walking, forgetting that, with the sun behind you, the backs of your legs and your neck are getting badly sunburnt. Pushing through prickly vegetation in shorts isn't fun either. Always carry long trousers and a long-sleeved shirt and put them on when you have had enough sun, and *always* wear a sunhat. Choose a shady spot for your lunch on hot days, and make sure that you carry with you a good supply of fruit and water.

Where to stay

If you want to stay by the sea, there is no more interesting place than **Viana do Castelo**. From here you can do all the walks in the book, provided that you have a car and are prepared to drive significant distances each day. There are also excellent places inland, along the river Lima, which are situated closer to the main walking area. About 25km along the Lima Valley lies **Ponte de Lima**, a town of considerable character which offers limited hotel accommodation but has many 'Turismo de Habitação' establishments in the vicinity (manor houses; see web details on page 49). Even further inland lie **Ponte da Barca** (42km) and **Arcos de Valdevez** (48km), both smaller than Ponte de Lima, but of even greater charm. Both offer tourist accommodation and are well situated for access to our walks.

Weather
A walking holiday in northern Portugal is not recommended before April. Not that April is a settled month — you can expect anything from warm sunny days to showers, days of rain or even occasional cold, biting winds — but usually April offers plenty of walking opportunities. The weather settles more in May, when it starts to get hotter, but occasional rain may still be encountered — especially late in the afternoon in the mountains. June sees the temperature rising steadily, until it becomes too hot to walk — almost certainly by the second half of the month. The summer heat starts to fade sometime in September, and walking opportunities return again, lasting throughout October — but now with an increasing risk of rainy days. Winter is characterised by a fairly high rainfall, but there can be periods of clear settled weather; splendid walking for those of us who live locally, but impossible to predict and arrange a visit from overseas.

Things that bite or sting
Dogs can be a nuisance. You may find carrying a 'Dog Dazer' reassuring. This small, easily portable ultrasonic device emits a noise which is inaudible to the human ear, but startles aggressive dogs and persuades them to back off. Contact Sunflower Books, who sell them. The best advice otherwise, if you feel threatened and have no walking stick, is to pick up a stone and pretend to throw it. More often than not, the dogs bark loudly but are rarely aggressive. Rabies is absent in Portugal, so should you be unfortunate enough to get bitten, at least feel reassured concerning this. You should nevertheless get bites properly treated at the nearest 'Centro de Saúde' (Health Centre).

Snakes are something you will have to be on your guard against. They tend to be drowsier and less likely to move out of your way in spring; in summer they are usually livelier and slither away. Most are probably harmless but, if there are any of the viper species around, great care is needed. Most snakes are more frightened of you than you are of them, and will move out of your way rapidly; if they don't, the best advice is to move quietly out of their way. The real danger comes if you accidentally step on one. For this reason, it is *imperative* that you do not walk in the countryside in open sandals, no matter how comfortable they are for walking. Always have your feet and ankles well covered, and it is a sensible precaution to wear your long trousers tucked into your socks. Take special care near water, when you are about to sit down, or when you choose to rest your hand, so unthinkingly, on a drystone wall. Most pharmacies now sell anti-venom kits.

Scorpions are around, too, but you are most likely to see them in the height of summer, when they are usually seeking shade; so don't leave any of your clothing on the ground. Accidentally turning over rocks or stones may expose them but, generally, they offer no serious threat; their sting is more painful than danger-ous for most people.

In areas which are well forested or where there is thick undergrowth, **ticks** can be a problem. As you brush through woodlands, broom and gorse, they can get onto your clothes but, if you follow our advice about wearing long trousers and a long-sleeved shirt, you should be able to keep them off your skin. If they do manage to get to your skin, it is necessary to make them withdraw before you take them off. An easy way to do this is to touch them with methylated spirits or petrol.

Bees and wasps are around in summer, so make sure you carry the necessary creams and pills, especially if you are allergic to insect bites. **Mosquitoes** can be a nuisance, especially in hotel rooms on hot summer nights, just when you want a window open to get some fresh air! Electric plug-in repellers (available in most supermarkets) are quite effective, but should only be used with an open window.

Portuguese for walkers

Outside the main resorts, few people speak English. If you want to ask directions in the country-side, you may well need to try your hand at Portuguese. A good technique is to memorise the key questions and all their possible answers given below; **then always phrase your question to elicit either a 'yes' (sim/** pronounced **sengh) or 'no' (não/naough) answer.**

Key questions

English	*Portuguese*	*approximate pronunciation*
'Pardon me,	Faz o favor,	**Fahz** oh fah-**vohr**,
sir (madam).	senhor(senhora).	s ehn-**yohr**(sehn-**yoh**-rah).
Where is	Onde é	**Ohn**-deh **eh**
the path to ...	o trilho para ...	oh tree-lyoh pah-**rah** ...
the road to ...	a estrada para ...	ah ish-**trah**-dah **pah**-rah ...
the way to ...	o caminho para ...	oh cah-**mee**-noh **pah**-rah ...
the bus stop?	a paragem?	ah pah-rah-**jeng**?
Many thanks.	Muito obrigado.	**Mween**-toh oh-bree-**gah**-doh.
	(a woman says	
	muito obrigada)	(oh-bree-**gah**-<u>dah</u>)

Possible answers

English	*Portuguese*	*approximate pronunciation*
Here	aqui	ah-**key**
There	ali	ah-**lee**
Straight ahead	sempre em frente	**sem**-preh em **frenght**
Behind	atrás	ah-**trahsh**
To the right	a direita	ah deh-**ray**-tah
To the left	a esquerda	ah ish-**kehr**-dah
Above	em cima	engh **see**-mah
Below	em baixo	engh **biesh**-oh

Try to get a native speaker (possibly someone at the hotel or a taxi driver) to help you learn the pronunciation. You must pronounce very carefully the name of your destination. For guidance with the pronunciation of a place names in this book, see the Index on page 132.

When you have your mini-speech memorised, always ask the many questions that you can concoct from it in such a way that a yes/no answer will result. Never ask an open-ended question such as 'Where is the main road?' and leave it at that! Unless you are actually standing on it, you will not understand the answer! Instead, ask the question, then **suggest the most likely answer yourself**, for example:

> 'Faz o favor, senhora. Onde é a estrada para Porto? É sempre em frente?' or 'Faz o favor, senhor. Onde é o trilho para Trapela? É em cima a esquerda?'

If you go through your list of answers, you will eventually get a yes — with a vigorous nod of the head — and it will be a lot more reliable than just sign language.

This village of ruined abrigos, *Branda de Berzavo, a testimony to the time when these hills were used extensively for summer pastures, is seen on Walks 7 and 8. Isolated* abrigos *continue to be maintained in the higher areas, but gone are the days when whole villages were needed.*

An inexpensive phrase book is a very valuable aid from which you can choose other 'key' phrases and answers. Remember, too, that it is always friendly to greet people you may meet on your walks with a 'good morning' or 'good afternoon' (bom dia/**bohm dee**-ah) or (boa tarde/**boah tar**-day).

We do use some local terminology in the descriptions and, to avoid repetition in the walk notes, below is a list of these **local words** and their meaning:

Abrigo	a rough stone-built shelter, most commonly found in the uplands (photographs above and on pages 40 and 96)
Espigueiro	a stone or wooden structure for storing maize; usually on 'toadstool' supports and with slatted wooden or stone side walls (photographs pages 88, 108-109)
Eira	a flat, paved area used for drying and flailing maize; frequently these are found near the *espigueiros*

Organisation of the walks

The walks in this book are largely focused on the central and northern areas of the Peneda-Gerês National Park. You might begin by considering the large fold-out touring map inside the back cover. Here you can see at a glance the overall terrain, the road network and the location of the various routes. Quickly flipping through the pages, you will find that there is at least one photograph for each walk. Having selected one or two potential excursions from the map and the photographs, look over the planning information at the beginning of each walk. Here you'll find walking times, grade, equipment and how to get there and return. If the grade and equipment specifications are beyond your scope, don't despair! There's almost always a short or alternative version of the walk and, in most cases, these are less demanding of ability and equipment.

When you turn to the walking notes, you'll find that the text begins with an introduction — to give you the flavour of the walk, and a comment on special points of interest. The route is then described in detail. The text is supplemented by large-scale maps (all at a scale of 1:40,000).

Note that the times given are **neat walking times** and include only brief pauses, where you might stop to recover breath. They do *not* include photographic or picnic stops, or *any* stop of indeterminate length. ***Add at least 50 percent to the total time shown at the top of the walk and, if you prefer to walk at a leisurely pace, double it.*** There are many time checks in the text, but these are *not* intended to be matched minute-by-minute throughout the walk. The most reliable way to use the book is to note the ***time difference*** to the next point on the route. Don't forget to take transport connections at the end of the walk into account, particularly if you are meeting a taxi or friends. (As a reminder, we have put in a suggested time allowance for most of the main walks.) The most important factor is consistency of walking times, and we have made an effort to check our times at least twice. You'll soon see how your pace compares with ours and make adjustments for your stride ... and the heat!

Many of the **symbols** used on the walking maps are self-explanatory, but below is a key to the most important:

motorway	spring, waterfall, etc	railway station
main road	— 400 — height (50 m intervals)	castle, fort
secondary road	watermill	specified building
motorable route	church.chapel	quarry, mine
track	shrine or cross	stadium
path, trail	cemetery	*abrigos* village
main walk	picnic tables	campsite
alternative walk	best views	picnic suggestion (see pages 10-13)
walk on watercourse	bus stop	
	car parking	map continuation

Walk 1: SERRA DE ARGA (MONTARIA • ALTO DAS COCANHAS • PEDRULHOS • MONTARIA)

See also photo pages 10-11
Distance: 11.8km/7.3mi; 2h57min (allow 5h)
Grade: moderate-strenuous. There is a climb of 250m/820ft initially, followed by a descent, then another climb of 150m/ 490ft to the highest point. The tracks and trails used are mainly good, but there are some short difficult sections.
Equipment: sturdy shoes or boots, long-sleeved shirt, long trousers, sunglasses, binoculars, suncream, fleece, raingear, picnic, water
Transport: ⊟ Access is from the N305, the road between Lanheses and Âncora. Heading north along this road from the crossroads at Lanheses (0km), pass through Vilar de Murteda and, as the road levels off, turn right (8.2km) to the sign-posted village of São Lourenço Montaria. On reaching the village keep ahead to the pleasantly shady central square (9.7km) with the church and 'Junta Freguesia' (Parish Council Office); park in front of the latter. Montaria itself is an attractive village and well worth exploring.
Short walks: both are easy; equipment and transport as the main walk
1 Montaria — Viveiro Florestal — Montaria (7.7km/ 4.8mi; 1h59min). Follow the main walk to the 1h05min-point, then keep straight ahead. Stay on this track to head back to the Viveiro

Florestal. Cross the bridge and walk up the road, to the junction at the 2min-point.
2 Montaria — Viveiro Florestal — watermills — Montaria (4.6km/2.9mi; 1h05min). Instead of turning right at the 2min-point, keep ahead, walking down to the Viveiro Florestal (7min). Cross the bridge and head left uphill on a forestry track. 20min from the Viveiro, just before the forestry track swings round left towards some pine trees, turn right on a path with red and yellow waymarks. Head up over a small pass (31min), then descend steeply into the valley beyond. There are plenty of rock pools and stopping places ahead, as well as watermills hidden in the undergrowth. The path continues downhill on the right-hand side of the stream (after 38min without waymarks), until you come to an open area with pines and a stone wall (48min). Follow the stone wall round to the right, to come to a trail (52min) which takes you back to the Viveiro (58min). Now retrace your outward route to Montaria (1h05min).
Longer walk: São João d'Arga (15.9km/9.9mi; 4h09min; fairly strenuous, with total ascents of 600m/ 1970ft). Follow the main walk to the 1h27min-point, then see the panel on page 62 to include this detour in the main walk.

The Serra de Arga is a small but striking range of mountains on the north side of the river Lima between Viana do Castelo and Ponte de Lima. Composed of granite, and with a treeless summit reaching almost 800m, it looks like a huge barren flat-topped mound, but it has the distinction of being highly visible for miles around. This walk will show you that the Serra de Arga is not as barren as it appears from a distance. Right from the start, you climb through woods, and further on encounter old watermills dotted along the streams. As you climb higher the landscape becomes harsher, with granite peaks and tors providing a natural exhibition of surreal sculptures. At the highest point on the main walk you will get extensive views down to the coast. From here you could take a detour to an interesting old monastery, São João d'Arga, before returning and rejoining the main route. The last stretch takes you alongside a beautiful gorge on the river Âncora.

In 2h47min you're surrounded by lush greenery, as the path runs above a pretty gorge carrying the Âncora River.

Start the walk from the village square in **Montaria** (283m): head up the cobbled road with a white and red waymark, to the left of the JUNTA FREGUESIA. When you come to a tarmac road within two minutes, turn right. *(But for Short walk 2, keep ahead here.)* Two minutes later, just after a 'SERVIÇOS FLORES-TAIS' sign, turn right on a way-marked track (**4min**). Initially the track is broken tarmac but soon, as you turn in left above some forestry cottages (**6min**), you are on a grassy trail. Half a minute later, turn left in front of a WATER TANK and climb steadily up the wooded hillside, away from the village, now on a mainly granite-paved trail.

The trail levels off again briefly (**14min**), and here you begin to get extensive views down to the coast and Vila Praia de Âncora. Pass a small WATER TANK on the left (**19min**) and in another couple of minutes head into mimosa woodland. In **25min** keep on ahead, ignoring the waymarked path off to the right. A minute later, bear left, dropping down slightly onto a grassy trail, where you will continue walking on the level. Ahead you enjoy views over to the valley and higher ground which feature later in the walk.

Having passed a distinctive rocky outcrop on your left, you rise gently up to meet a road (**31min**), where you turn left downhill. The road takes you down past a sharp left-hand bend (**36min**). Some 250m/ yds past this bend (**40min**), turn right downhill on a rough track. Bear right again after 100m and continue downhill to a stream (**Regueiro dos Enxurros; 44min**). This is a pleasant, shaded spot for picnics, with an excellent rock pool for swimming just 20m upstream.

Cross the stream and follow the white arrow pointing you uphill to the right, taking a rough track round the hillside. The track levels out (**48min**) and you now contour round the hillside, towards the head of a valley, crossing another stream on a bend (**Regueiro da Lapa Ladrão; 57min**). The track continues on the other side of this valley and leads you round to the beginning of a large open area (**1h03min**). Notice a small STONE BRIDGE on the left as you come into this flat area.

Take care two minutes later. You need to find a path leading off to the right; there is a small cairn opposite it and another on the corner, while the track ahead is almost at the top of a gentle rise. Turn right onto this grassy footpath (**1h 05min**), heading towards THREE STANDING STONES on the **Alto das Cocanhas**, each about 1m/3ft high. Just over a minute later, before reaching the stones, turn right as you meet an obvious crossing trail, to head into the jaws of a deep, barren and stony valley. After crossing a STREAM (**1h11min**), you come to a delightful old trail, paved in giant granite slabs. This trail is waymarked too — in double stripes of red upon yellow. The route now takes you steeply up through a valley where granite dominates, to create a compelling landscape — barren and bleak, but not entirely without vegetation. Soon, looking ahead at the huge granite tors, you might just spot one resembling a tortoise.

At the point where the STONE TRAIL ENDS and becomes a dirt trail dropping down to near-level terrain (**1h27min**), look out for a path off to the left (it's faint initially) and follow this up the hillside to the left.*

---

*But if you are doing the longer walk to São João d'Arga, keep right here, and turn to page 62 to continue.

São João d'Arga

The monastery of São João d'Arga nestles in a wooded valley on the north side of the Serra de Arga and makes a worthwhile out-and-back extension to the main walk. Follow the main walk to the 1h27min-point but, instead of turning left uphill, carry on round to the right. Sometimes you will have to negotiate some slightly boggy stretches (growing amongst the mosses around here is the fly-eating *Drosera rotundifolia*, but it needs a good eye and a careful search to find it). You will emerge on the old trail again and reach the top of a pass (**9min**). The view behind you, down to the Lima Valley and the sea, is reason enough to pause for breath. Here you cross over a track and continue straight on down towards the monastery along the way-marked trail.

The protection of the valley allows the vegetation to grow tall again and, shortly, a spinney of fire-damaged pines is passed as you descend. Notice (**16min**) a second, similar valley over to the right, and be sure not to confuse it with this one on your return. You enter a birch woodland (**23min**), and soon you may spot the blue-flowered *Omphalodes nitida*. As you emerge into a clearing (**27min**), turn left to join the surfaced road. Turn right and cross the bridge. Follow the road into a gentle climb, but where the road bends right two minutes later, continue ahead to the abandoned monastery of **São João d'Arga** (**32min**). Many of the granite-built cloisters remain intact, and the monastery is still the site of annual pilgrimages in August. To return, retrace your steps up the valley to the track at the top of the pass. Cross it and rejoin the main walk at the 1h27min-point (**1h12min**).

There are no waymarks at this stage, but the path will lead you to the top of a small pass (**1h34min**). The views from here to the west and the Atlantic demand a pause as you recover your breath from the last short ascent.

From now on it's almost all downhill! You drop over the pass onto a fine granite trail with occasional yellow waymarks. You pass an old watercourse off to the left (**1h49min**); this was designed to channel water round the hillside for irrigation and to drive the watermills. Carry on downhill, still on granite pavement, until you meet a

Most of the streams flowing off the Serra de Arga have watermills, some, like this one near the 2h47min-point, still working today.

track just below the first house of **Pedrulhos** (**2h03min**). This house seems to have dozens of dogs, but they are all securely chained!

Accompanied no doubt by the canine cacophony, turn sharp left below this house on a footpath. This leads in one minute to a SMALL DAM, where you take the footpath down to the right. Cross over a SMALL BRIDGE and then head up a granite-cobbled track to the left (*ignore* the yellow arrows pointing right) and you will quickly be on a dirt track. The track takes you out to a tarmac road (**2h21min**), which you follow to the left. Straight away you pass a turning left to the old school; take the *next* left, after about 100m/yds, heading up a granite-cobbled track (at this point the tarmac bends right downhill). You pass alongside a wavy BRICK WALL on the right as you walk into the village of **Trás-Âncora**. After 300m/yds, by a lamppost, turn left at a T-junction, still on granite cobbles.

The route takes you round a small valley. On the far side you pass in front of a house with large plate glass windows. Continue until this granite track drops down to a tarmac road (**2h33min**), just by a small SHRINE in the wall on the left. Turn left on the tarmac, cross a bridge (**2h38min**) and immediately pass a STONE CROSS on the right. Look for a path up left, some 50m/yds beyond the bridge and follow this uphill. This path rises quite steeply

above a beautiful gorge carrying the **Âncora River**. At the top of the path (**2h47min**) you enjoy fine views down over waterfalls. Here the path joins a dirt track. Our route is ahead and slightly left, but first make a small detour to the right (*not included in the main walk times*). You will come to a tarmac road in two minutes — with a lovely group of old watermills and, just along the road to the left, a welcoming café with splendid views from its patio.

From the 2h47min-point follow the dirt track ahead into the pines, ignoring the waymarked turn to the left. Almost immediately you come to a large clearing with a BANDSTAND and CHAPEL (note the fascinating inscription on the chapel door). Carry on along a cobbled track on the far side of the clearing; this leads you through fields and down to the paved road. Turn left on the road and walk back to the square in **Montaria** (**2h57min**).

Walk 2: SERRA DE ARGA (ARGA DE BAIXO • PORTA DO LOBO • ARGA DE CIMA • ARGA DE BAIXO)

See also photograph page 2
Distance: 13.7km/8.5mi; 2h24min *(allow 4.5h)*
Grade: easy-moderate. The going underfoot is generally easy and the ascent of 250m/820ft in the first half of the walk a steady plod. Note that there is very little shade en route.
Equipment: sturdy shoes or boots, long-sleeved shirt, long trousers, sunglasses, suncream, fleece, raingear, picnic, water
Transport: 🚌 from either Viana do Castelo or Ponte de Lima take the N202 to Santa

Comba (0km). Now follow the signs to Serra de Arga, passing through Moreira do Lima. At 6.5km be sure to turn left towards Arga. The road rises steeply past the villages of Cerquido and Arga de Cima. When you reach Arga de Baixo (16km), park by the church and bandstand.
Short walks: There are no easy ways of shortening this walk. But there are shorter waymarked walks in the area, details of which can be obtained from the Interpretation Centre at Arga de Baixo.

This walk offers some remarkable contrasts, but they appear gradually and are very much related to the altitude at which you are walking. The altitude in turn is a reflection of the geology — the granite highland and the schist lowland. Having taken you steadily up to the bare, open expanses of the Serra de Arga at 750m, the walk leads you round to the eastern edge of this plateau — to the wonderful vantage point of Porta do Lobo (Wolf's Pass). From here you walk steadily down off the granite highland, to pass through some fascinating villages and hamlets. Here it is easy to see how traditional architecture has been directly influenced by the contrasting rock type forming the lower ground.

This very basic footbridge, the Pontão de Lobo, is encountered just after the 2h-point. Tradition has it that it was built to enable the padre to walk more easily between parishes on his way to celebrating mass.

Start the walk at **Arga de Baixo** (483m): with your back to the CHURCH, turn right up the road and climb away from the village. You will come to a left turn (**4min**) which leads up to the INTERPRETATION CENTRE; this is worth visiting,

Blocks of quartzite and slabs of schist combine attractively in this drystone wall seen at the 1h51min-point — resulting in a 'warmer' colour than is seen in much of the Minho, where granite is the only stone available.

especially if you are going to spend more time near the Serra de Arga and want details of more walks. Continue up the road; as it levels off, you will get excellent views ahead and over the Minho Valley to Spain. Turn left off the road (**16min**) on a rough track. (Continuing ahead on the road for 1km would bring you down to the monastery of São João d'Arga; see Walk 1.) This track rises steadily. At the point where it levels off briefly (**28min**), ignore the rough track off to the right. Continue climbing up to a junction at **Alto da Portela (44min)**, where you take the track to the left. Still climbing steadily, you eventually emerge on an extensive PLATEAU area near the top of the **Serra de Arga** — at about 750m above sea level (**58min**). Ahead in the distance you will see some slightly higher hills and radio masts, but what impresses is the expanse and silence of this upland pasture. As you continue along the track you will become aware of countless stonechats and skylarks, while buzzards are frequently seen overhead. There are also large herds of *garrano* horses to be found, free to roam on this ancient land.

At the end of a long straight section (**1h05min**), look out for some isolated rocks just off to the right of the track. Just past these rocks, the track curves round to the right. Take a path which turns left off this bend, heading up the shallow grassy valley ahead (running in the same direction as the long straight section you have just

After walking across the top of the Serra de Arga, the path leads you to the eastern edge of the plateau at Porta do Lobo. Notice the cart wheel ruts in the pavement (below) and the red and yellow waymarking (left). This is a good spot to have lunch, enjoying the views down to Ponte de Lima and the mountains of the national park further inland.

walked along). There are a couple of pine trees on the skyline at the top of this valley. Initially the path is grassy, but soon (**1h09min**) you rise onto a granite pavement with red and yellow waymarking on the rocks ahead. You pass the TWO PINE TREES you saw when you first turned off the track (**1h12min**) and continue through a rocky area.

After crossing a small COL (**1h16min**), the path descends into a lovely secluded valley, at the far end of which you can see a group of pine trees. When you reach these PINES (and a small enclosure; **1h 22min**), bear left — towards the back of a SIGNPOST. Just beyond the signpost and round to the left you will see more red and yellow waymarks: follow these onto a granite pavement (deeply rutted by years of passing ox-cart wheels; see bottom photograph opposite). The rutted pavement crests **Porta do Lobo** (750m; **1h23min**). This natural rock shelter (top photograph opposite), with fabulous views towards the Lima Valley and down over Ponte de Lima far below, is an ideal picnic spot … and from now on the walk is all downhill!

From this pass you have a steady descent on the granite pavement, always with cairns and waymarks. After crossing a small flat area, you drop down to a small stream (**Regato da Fraga; 1h31min**) and enjoy your first views over to Arga de Baixo 3km ahead. The trail shortly pulls away onto the right-hand side of the valley, eventually descending to the WALLED ENCLOSURES and WATERMILLS at **Souteiro** (**1h 45min**). Follow the trail

between the enclosures and notice, after about a minute, a change in the colour and texture of the rock you are walking over. You are passing from granite (which forms the high ground behind you) onto schist and quartzite, which forms the lower ground ahead.

Meeting a granite-cobbled track at a T-junction in front of a house (**1h47min**), turn left, walking between drystone walls. You pass an *espigueiro* on the right made from schist (**1h48min**); the style is quite different from the granite *espigueiros* seen on most of the other walks, a reflection of the different stone used. Schist is far less suitable than granite for sculpting and carving. In another minute, at a junction with a stone-paved road, bear left (note the interesting carvings around the windows in the ruin on the left here, shown in the photograph below).

Pass a group of POSTBOXES on the left (**1h51min**) and ignore the turning right downhill just past them. You will notice now how all the older buildings and walls here in **Arga de Cima**

Carvings on the ruin passed at the 1h49min-point

use the mix of local stone to great effect, giving a texture and softness that is a refreshing contrast to the granite seen throughout much of the Minho.

Take care to bear left opposite a small house with two MODEL WINDMILLS on posts (**1h 54min**); the granite-paved road swings right here, but you need to take the rough granite track leading down past old houses. You shortly come to a house built partly into rock on the right. Just after this, on a right hand bend, there is an IRON GATE on the left. Keep on the track, *ignoring* this gate. But almost immediately, *do* turn left — through a METAL GATE (there is a waymarked lamp post just *beyond* it). You join a grassy trail, descend past an *espigueiro* and *eira* on the left, and come into woodland.

Meeting a granite-paved road (**1h59min**), go though the DOUBLE GATE just up to the right. Then immediately turn left uphill on a path to the church. Pass round and above the CHURCH AND CEMETERY, then take the rough path down to a STREAM (**2h01min**). Turn right here on a rough trail. Just 20m/yds up this trail you come to a drystone wall leading left, back down to the stream. It's worth making a small diversion back down to the stream here, to see the small footbridge shown on page 64.

Then return up to the rough trail and follow the line of TELEPHONE POLES to the top of the next rise. Off to the left is a small rocky knoll, where you will see the traditional beehive, made from cork, shown on page 2. Apiculture is still widely practised in the area,

and the honey produced is usually full of flavour from the abundant heather and wild flowers.

Bearing round to the left, still following the TELEPHONE POSTS, you cross an old STONE BRIDGE (**2h06min**). Note the two WATERMILLS with interesting stone-built mill-races. Continue up the road into **Gândara**. Circle to the right of a WATER TANK, then bear left past the POSTBOXES on the left (**2h08min**). Follow a granite-paved road with waymarked lamp posts down to a STONE BRIDGE (**2h09min**). Turn uphill and left a minute later, still on a granite road. Pass a new house on the left at the top of the rise and then turn right immediately, past a house with lots of noisy (but kennelled) dogs.

Just past the dogs start to descend below vines on a granite trail (**2h12min**); all is peace again when you reach an open area with another trail coming in from the left (**2h15min**). Carry on round to the right, to a granite-paved road by 'Casa do Marco' (**2h17min**). Follow this road round to the left, shortly passing under vines and noting the old *eira* and *espigueiros* off to the right (**2h20min**). Here the houses and walls are once more of granite.

As the granite-paved road swings round to the right (and slightly uphill; **2h21min**), take the grassy trail ahead to the left, descending slightly, into a small valley. Two minutes later a granite pavement comes underfoot; this leads up to a T-junction with a tarmac road. A café is opposite. Turn left and walk back to the CHURCH in **Arga de Baixo** (**2h24min**).

Agriculture and landscape

When one looks out over the Minho countryside one cannot fail to be impressed by the amount of work that has gone into fashioning the landscape as it is today. The steep terraces, the stone walls running over hillsides, the granite-paved tracks leading to fields and to upland pastures, the small enclosures and vineyards that 'fit' so perfectly into the contours of the land, all combine to create a landscape of great beauty, harmony and interest. It is a living landscape too. With every season the same view will

The grape harvest (vindima) *is one of the busiest times of the year and is frequently a race against time as the summer ends and the fickle Minho autumn sets in.*

The traditional upland agricultural system relies on careful, balanced management of what nature offers. In the picture above you can see how the hilltops are still 'cropped' for cattle bedding which, after the winter, is turned out onto the fields (far right) immediately adjacent to the village. The barrosã cattle are a fundamental part of this system and, as such, are highly valued, being taken out to the pasture for daily grazing (above right). When not in the fields or working, they will be back in the cowshed (right) preparing the next load of compost!

change dramatically; there will be changes even from one week to the next. The local farmers are always doing something in their fields to ensure this.

It is worth putting what we see today into an historical context. This landscape would have been quite different 300 years ago. Before the introduction of maize from the Americas, the land could support only a very small population, living off and working the lower land of the valleys. At this time much of the higher ground would have been forested, with little or no farming. One of the biggest problems was the absence of a cereal (and hence flour for bread) that could be stored through the humidity of the Minho winter without going mildewed.

Maize transformed this. The corn on the cob could be stored in *espigueiros* (see pages 108-109), the grain stores so typical of the area, that are seen on almost all our walks. Their design is simple but functional; the slit sidewalls of granite or wood allowing air to circulate, the toadstool supports preventing vermin from entering. There are variants of this, for example the wickerwork *canastros* (shown overleaf) and

Spreading compost, near Cutelo (Walk 5). The mounds of black compost piled across fields is a common sight in the spring. There is a wonderful harmony in this: the ox carts carry bedding down from the hilltops, and the winter's bedding is then turned out onto the fields as in this picture, ready to provide the goodness for another crop of maize, which in turn will provide straw and fodder for the oxen.

the different 'architecture' resulting from use of a different type of stone, as seen on Walk 2 at Arga de Baixo. Usually in front, or nearby the *espigueiro,* will be an area of flat rock, the *eira,* used for drying and flailing.

But maize had far more impact on the landscape than just *espigueiros.* Suddenly the Minho could support a much bigger population; there was a population explosion and pressure to grow ever more of the new crop. Pressure on land meant that vines, previously growing across fields, were pushed to the perimeter to make space for maize. More marginal land, higher up the hills and valleys, was brought under cultivation, frequently by building terraces. Many of the smaller villages and hamlets on higher ground were established in the latter stages of this expansion, in the second half of the 17th century. Then

came the widespread use of the magnificent long-horned *barrosã* cow as a draft animal. These are still prized for the quality of their meat, and indeed there were regular exports from Viana to England in the 18th century (along with brisk trade in codfish imports and wine exports). Strangely, little dairy produce comes from these cattle, more from the slightly lighter-built *cachena* cows.

Subsequently a system of farming developed which survives to this day and which is based on a wonderfully balanced use of the local resources. On the higher ground there is abundant growth of broom, heather and gorse. This is harvested and then transported in ox-carts down to the villages to be used as cattle bedding. This in turn is carried down to the fields in spring and used as compost, ploughed in prior to sowing

71

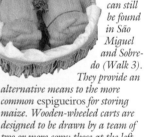

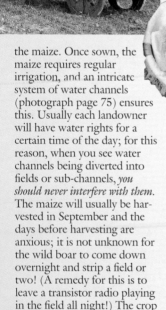

the maize. Once sown, the maize requires regular irrigation, and an intricate system of water channels (photograph page 75) ensures this. Usually each landowner will have water rights for a certain time of the day; for this reason, when you see water channels being diverted into fields or sub-channels, *you should never interfere with them.* The maize will usually be harvested in September and the days before harvesting are anxious; it is not unknown for the wild boar to come down overnight and strip a field or two! (A remedy for this is to leave a transistor radio playing in the field all night!) The crop is cut and transported, intact, back to the *eira,* where the family will sit around in a group for the *esfolhadas* (removing the outer leaves from the cob). This is a great occasion (usually reserved for the evenings) for chat, banter

Canastros (top left) can still be found in São Miguel and Sobre-do (Walk 3). They provide an alternative means to the more common espigueiros *for storing maize. Wooden-wheeled carts are designed to be drawn by a team of two or more cows; those at the left are used for collecting grapes. Above: flax — drying in the fields (top), being beaten in the traditional way, using a wooden blade against cork (middle), and the end product, linen thread*

and clearing the remaining stock of the previous year's *vinho* to make space for the impending new harvest. To add spice to the occasion, any young lad who peels open a brown or red cob (called a *rei,* or 'king') can claim a kiss from the lass of his choice in the workgroup.

Nothing is wasted from the harvest. The maize stalks are

stored in ricks for subsequent use as cattle fodder. Even the husks of the cobs are used as cattle food. The cobs are traditionally dried, stored and eventually flailed. The resultant corn is then milled, traditionally in one of the watermills that are found throughout the region (photograph page 63), although today most farmers have an electric mill in their basement. Maize bread (broa) is normally baked about every two weeks; it stores successfully up to this period.

Other crops important to the traditional way of life are potatoes, cabbages, beans and onions. Flax is still grown, processed and spun into linen thread for subsequent weaving. Some home-embroidered linen is of exceptional quality. A good place to see this being spun and woven is at Brufe (Walks 5 and 6).

Apart from cattle, most families would keep a pig and fatten this up for the winter kill (matança). The meat would be salted down for use throughout the year. Delicious sausages (chouriço) would be smoked over the open fire to later on provide hearty snacks (with broa and wine) during work in the fields.

Obviously viniculture forms a central part of the agricultural activity. The vines, on their often lofty trellises (photograph page 120), are pruned back heavily in the winter months. From spring, right the way through to the harvest the vines will be sprayed about every two weeks (traditionally with copper sulphate) to eliminate fungal infections that can thrive in the humid climate. The harvest (vindima) usually occurs two or three

weeks after the maize has been gathered in. This is another time of great collective activity, the roads and tracks congested with grape-laden carts. It is not uncommon to see tractor and trailer queues several hundred metres long waiting to discharge their loads at the co-operatives.

Although most farmers will sell into the co-operative, many still produce just for their own consumption, frequently still treading the grapes in the traditional way. The grape must is subsequently fermented and distilled to produce bagaceira, a local form of aguardente.

The new wine will be tasted and first consumed at the time of the chestnut harvest (São Martinho) when there is a traditional feast, or magusto. If you are offered some local wine during your walks, do try it; drunk in the village environment, it is surprisingly good and not too alcoholic! The chances are you will be handed the wine in a small bowl, probably accompanied with some broa and chouriço.

Rural depopulation in recent years has resulted in significant areas of more marginal land falling into disuse. And so the traditional way of working with cattle-drawn ploughs and carts is disappearing. While much of the work is now mechanised, you will still find farmers using the traditional methods, especially in the remoter areas of our walks. Here it is still quite easy to find the ox carts being pulled by the sturdy barrosã cattle linked together with the beautifully carved yokes, perpetuating a way of life that maize brought to these hills 300 years ago.

Walk 3: SÃO MIGUEL • SOBREDO • GERMIL • FROUFE • SÃO MIGUEL

See also photographs on pages 34, 41, 72
Distance: 16.6km/10.3mi; 4h37min (*allow 6h*)
Grade: strenuous; a fairly long walk, with a stiff climb on the approach to Germil and a total height gain of just over 600m/1970ft
Equipment: sturdy shoes or boots, long-sleeved shirt, long trousers, sunglasses, suncream, fleece, raingear, picnic, water
Transport: 🚌 from Ponte da Barca (note km reading) take the road towards Lindoso. Some 11km beyond Ponte da Barca the road drops down to cross a bridge over an inlet of the Touvedo Reservoir. Immediately beyond this bridge turn right (signposted to Germil and Ermida). Pass the café

Novas Pontes on your left and come into São Miguel (also known as 'Entre-Ambos-os-Rios'); park on the left, just beyond the cemetery (12.8km).
Short walks: For an easier grade walk choose from:
1 São Miguel — Sobredo — São Miguel (4.8km/3mi; 1h10min; easy). Follow the main walk to Sobredo and return the same way.
2 São Miguel — Sobredo — water channel below Germil — São Miguel (10.6km/6.6mi; 3h10min; moderate). This variant avoids the steepest section of the walk. Follow the main walk to the end of the water channel (1h30min), and return the same way.

S obredo, Germil, São Miguel are names that roll easily off the tongue, and the images that spring to mind become magical with the passage of time. Time is the key, for these villages seem to have settled for an existence in an age long since past. Their granite houses, their farming methods, and their mode of life have changed little with the passing of years. But these villages are just an added bonus to a walk which explores a very scenic region. The route is partially waymarked with yellow dashes (a yellow cross means 'wrong way'). Unfortunately, the waymarks are not very frequent in the later stages (although some cairns help in the upper stretches) — so follow the notes carefully.

Start the walk at **São Miguel** (101m): from the car parking area head into the village. Within a minute turn right by a STONE CROSS, to continue wandering through the village in the direction of SOBREDO. Continue round to the left (**3min**), to pass a FOUNTAIN and tap on the right. *Canastros* (see page 72) are occasionally seen along this section of the route, but are left behind as

you move out of São Miguel. Notice too the old WATERMILL on the corner (**7min**), where a trail enters from the right — but our route continues along the cobbled road to the left here. The cobbled road rises to meet a tarred road (**10min**). Cross over and continue along a path which leads between woodland on the left and cultivated terraces to the right. Turn left as you emerge on the road again (**15min**) and enjoy a steady ascent through pine woodland. Meet a fork two minutes later, where you follow the signed route to the right, along the cobbled road towards SOBREDO. As you climb gently, views slowly open out to reveal a moun- tainous landscape with villages tucked away in the folds. The climbing becomes a little stiffer as you approach **Sobredo** (**33min**). Ignore the trail joining from the right and head into this fascinating old granite village, its texture softened only by the wooden-

This water channel, made out of granite slabs, is followed from just above Sobredo to just below Germil. The effort that must have gone into con- structing its 3.5km length indicates how vital a secure supply of water is.

sided *espigueiros* (see illustration and notes on pages 108-109) and the vine-covered pergola by which you leave. Keep on the cobbled road past a WASH-HOUSE on the right (**38min**). Two minutes later, as the cobbled road leads around to the left, keep ahead on a trail passing beneath vines and going by a modern house on the right.

As the trail divides three ways (**42min**), keep ahead up the centre trail in a gentle ascent, passing the FOOTBALL PITCH to your right and keeping ahead, over the small rise. You arrive on a granite-paved trail alongside a steep wooded valley down to the right. Just below lies a water channel and, even lower, another old trail is visible. Across the valley, extensively terraced hillsides are dwarfed by the mountains behind them.

There are some boggy areas to contend with (**51min**), as the trail descends diagonally to the right, but these can be negotiated by passing to the left. At the fork in the trail a minute later, keep up left on the major cobbled trail, to pass a WATERMILL on the left (**54min**). At the next fork, reached three minutes later, keep down right and continue around the bend, crossing a SLAB BRIDGE.

Soon, as you cross the bridge and rise up and over the WATER CHANNEL shown on page 75 (**1h**), turn right to walk alongside it. You now follow this channel for some 2km/1.25mi. The footpath is narrow in parts, and it is necessary to change sides at times to make progress, but the way is always interesting, with views over the **Rio de Germil**, and wild flowers closer at hand. Dwarf heather, *Erica umbellata*, with its umbels of dainty pink flowers, and the blue-flowered *Lithospermum diffusum* are just two of the species along the wayside.

As you near the river (**1h 30min**), just before the water channel bends around to the left, fork diagonally left up a path. This turn is waymarked but, if you miss it, you will simply come to a dead-end 30m/yds ahead, where the water channel takes its source in the river. Stony underfoot, the well-waymarked path follows the line of the river,

This typical stile (in Germil) illustrates well the use of available materials in everyday applications.

with fine views to its waterfalls and rock pools. You cross a tributary stream by a small stone *SLAB BRIDGE* (**1h35min**) and, almost immediately, follow the path to the left between this tributary and the main river. You climb away from the river, towards oak woodland, shortly crossing an old trail leading down towards the river. Within a minute the path leads back to the same old trail, which you now join to continue your ascent. Cross the stream to the left (**1h38min**) and then cross a *WATER CHANNEL*, to join a beautiful old granite trail. Keep left at the fork reached two minutes later, and stay ahead as a trail joins from the left. It is a steady uphill pull, as you can

judge when you see the river receding below you, but at least there is the advantage of shade in the leafy sections. The landscape is suddenly all soft greens (**1h48min**), as you look down onto the lovely old WATERMILL shown on page 34. It's beside a rushing stream. Another old trail joins from the left just before you swing right to cross a river by a stone SLAB BRIDGE two minutes later.

As you rise away from the trees, views open out over the wooded valley through which you have just walked. Keep ahead as a trail joins from the right (**1h58min**), and watch out for the traditional BEEHIVES nearby which are made from cork and thatch (like those seen on pages 2 and 85). Where the main trail swings away to the left (**2h02min**), turn right to follow the upper of two trails. It leads to a fork a minute later, where you keep left. Stay on this trail to enter **Germil de Baixo** (**2h10min**). Turn left just before the FOUNTAIN in the centre and continue, now on a cobbled road, up towards the main village. (It is worth a moment's diversion to the right just past the fountain, to see the wall-mounted ancient sundial on the left, with a Celtic face.)

Keep around to the right as you pass a CROSS and *espigueiro* on the left at the road junction (**2h13min**). As you enter **Germil** proper (630m), pass the Café Danaia on the left and almost immediately find an *espigueiro* on your right. Turn left here, following a cobbled road for one minute. Then turn sharp right uphill on a short granite path. This rises immediately to another granite-paved road, where you turn left. This road rapidly reduces to a granite trail. Keep ahead, ignoring the trail down left (**2h18min**), and you will come to a stream with a lovely old stone SLAB BRIDGE (**2h23min**). A minute later bear left, slightly downhill, to meet another trail rising from the left (**2h25min**). Follow this beautiful old granite pavement, contouring round the hillside, with ever more eye-catching views of Germil and its upland setting.

You will cross a couple of small streams and then, as the land-scape becomes bare and rocky, take the right fork (**2h40min**), to follow the trail to the highest point in this part of the walk — where it promptly ends by a small ruined *abrigo* (701m; **2h50min**). The views demand that you stop, at least for a moment, to gaze ahead, towards the Lima Valley, and left, to look back at Germil.

A path (initially faint) con-tinues from where the trail

Long-horned barrosã *cows and a hillside full of asphodels*

ends. Some CAIRNS lead you down towards the bottom of the valley; the lower part of the path is overgrown with heather and broom. Aim for the nearest part of the winter watercourse in this valley. Cross the WATERCOURSE (**2h55min**) and immediately on the other side you will find a large CAIRN. From the cairn rise diagonally to the left, along a narrow path, to climb slowly away from the valley floor, now following ample CAIRNS. As you rise to higher ground (**3h03min**), the cairns lead you over the shoulder of the hill and then diagonally down to the right, towards the next valley.

Soon (**3h10min**) the cairns will have led you down to a forestry track. Cross this, and you should find another CAIRN immediately below. Further cairns guide you down the hillside towards some walled enclosures which can be seen below. After crossing a small stream (an area called **Cabeças** on the map; **3h17min**), and just before the ENCLOSURES are reached, take the left fork. The path is faint initially, but it follows the stream and leads down to an old trail. Follow this trail along the left-hand side of the valley.

After passing under the PYLON LINES (**3h38min**), take care to swing slightly left into a depression with a WATER HOLE and small walled-in wooded area (by this time the trail has reduced to a footpath). Pick up a trail leading out of the small copse, immediately crossing a stream. Just after the stream crossing, turn left on a track (at an area called **Carrascos** on the map). This leads you downhill, parallel to the stream. Now,

with a drystone wall on your right, follow the track to a T-junction (where the wall ends). Turn left and ignore any turnings down to the right. You come into a wooded valley and cross a stream. Round the valley and, on the far side, as you leave the woodland, pass an electricity PYLON on the right. You are now heading due north. A forestry track comes in from the left, and soon you get your first views of Lourido and then Froufe below — as well as fine views to the west as you swing around the hillside at an area called **Mourinho**.

As the track starts to descend, turn sharp right on another track (**4h**) descending towards a FOOTBALL PITCH. Go past the pitch, then turn left immediately. Just one minute later, take a dirt track descending to the right. Just before reaching a house, turn sharp left (west) on a level footpath (**4h04min**). After just three minutes, turn sharp right downhill, past water pools and irrigation channels. On reaching some vines on trellises, turn right, dropping quickly to a tarmac road (**4h12min**).

Turn left on the road (or first get some refreshment at the Café Portela just up to the right). In another three minutes turn right downhill on a cobbled road, into **Froufe**. At the FOUNTAIN on the left (**4h26min**) keep round to the left, to rejoin the tarred road four minutes later. Keep right here, to return to the centre of **São Miguel** and the car parking area just beyond it (**4h37min**).

Walk 4: ERMIDA • BILHARES • ERMIDA

Distance: 8.5km/5.3mi; 2h
Grade: moderate. The climbing involved is a long and steady gain of 150m/490ft. There is a steep descent, which requires some agility. Walking, mostly on tracks and trails, is easy underfoot.
Equipment: sturdy shoes or boots, long-sleeved shirt, long trousers, sunglasses, suncream, fleece, raingear, picnic, water
Transport: 🚗 follow the car route from Ponte da Barca to São Miguel as described in Walk 3 (page 74). Drive through this village and follow the narrow road for a further 7.6km to reach Ermida. The route, a narrow tarmac surface with short cobbled sections, is cut into the steep sides of a valley for part of the way, and

not recommended for inexperienced or nervous drivers. Park by the cemetery on the left just as you reach Ermida.
Short walks: two particular points of interest are worth a short walk. Both are easy but require equipment as above.
1 Ermida — Bilhares — Ermida (4.8km/3mi; 1h12min). Go as far as the summer village of Bilhares and return the same way.
2 Ermida — bridge beyond Bilhares — Ermida (6.8km/4.25mi; 1h34min). Follow the main walk for 47min to reach the scenic old slab bridge beyond Bilhares (shown on page 83; a pleasant picnic spot); return the same way.

Situated at an altitude of around 500m/1650ft and connected to civilisation by the merest thread of a road, Ermida is one of the many hill villages which have developed and survived in isolation. Apart from spectacular scenery, this walk gives you a glimpse of the successful farming techniques which have been pursued

over centuries and which remain almost unchanged even today.

In a sense, Ermida is two villages. It is the one you meet where you park your car — the winter village — and the one you meet at a higher altitude later in the walk — Bilhares, the summer village. This seasonal transhumance was a way of life for many of the hill villagers throughout the mountainous northern region. Maize, introduced from America in the 16th and 17th centuries, was an important factor influencing this behaviour. By terracing the steep valley sides and by careful irrigation, it became possible to grow it in the hills (see, for example, the photograph on page 100). All the fertile land around the villages was pressed into use, displacing the cattle and forcing the herdsmen to take their animals to higher pastures. After sowing the maize in May, the villagers would take their cattle to pastures higher in the mountains and stay there with them until October. The summer villages are basic, to say the least. A typical house is built with granite walls and a thatched roof (see pages 84-85). But even in its simplicity, Bilhares seems luxury-class compared to the villages of *abrigos* encountered on other walks (for example, Walk 7). The story of maize is developed further in the section on agriculture (pages 69-73).

A lovely track takes you from Ermida, through the hillsides used for cultivation, up to Bilhares. As you pass

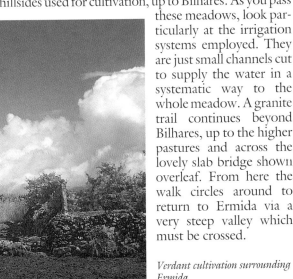

these meadows, look particularly at the irrigation systems employed. They are just small channels cut to supply the water in a systematic way to the whole meadow. A granite trail continues beyond Bilhares, up to the higher pastures and across the lovely slab bridge shown overleaf. From here the walk circles around to return to Ermida via a very steep valley which must be crossed.

Verdant cultivation surrounding Ermida

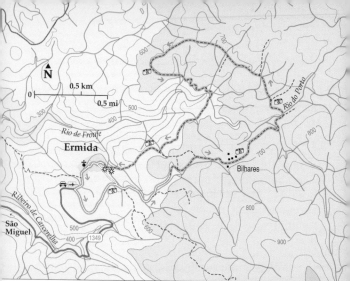

Start the walk from the
CEMETERY in **Ermida** (510m):
with your back to the cemetery, head up the cobbled
track. As soon as you gain a
little height there are fine views
overlooking the cultivated
terraces surrounding Ermida
which, in early summer, are a
lush and vibrant green (the
photograph on pages 80-81
was taken here). Keep ahead in
a gentle ascent, ignoring all

trails turning off left or right.
Soon after leaving Ermida,
keep an eye open for the
BEEHIVES made from a ring of
bark from the cork oak tree,
with a roof of thatch (shown
on page 85). A little later you'll
also spot some interesting
flowers in the meadows damp
from irrigation. Two orchids,
the common spotted orchid,
Dactylorhiza maculata, and
heart-flowered serapias, *Serapia*

cordigera, are most easily seen in the early summer months, before the grass gets too long. The track rises up and away from the stream on the right (**22min**). The age-old field irrigation technique shown opposite, using simple channels cut into the turf, is still in operation in the fields up ahead, and a good example can be seen as you look over the wall on the right (**28min**). Stay ahead, soon catching sight of the thatched granite houses shown overleaf, as you arrive at **Bilhares** (**36min**). After looking round the village, return to the old trail. Follow it up alongside the wall

Above: sheep crossing the old slab bridge (47min into the walk). Left: irrigation channels in the fields below Bilhares summer village. They are an effective way of ensuring a steady soaking of the ground which then produces the lush grass in spring. As a bonus, these pastures become a botanist's delight in the months of May and June, when you will see orchids like the common spotted orchid, Dactylorhiza maculata (opposite), and heart-flowered serapias, like Serapia pseudo-cordigera (below left).

on your left, still in steady ascent. Soon a deciduous wood lies over to the left. The aspect changes as you crest the rise (**40min**): gone are the green pastures, replaced by a rugged and hostile granite landscape which opens up before you. Cross a stream by the old SLAB BRIDGE shown above (**47min**) and, as you start to rise away from the stream on a trail, look for and follow another trail to the left two minutes later. It immediately crosses the **Rio do Porto**. Stay left when the trail divides (**53min**), and keep heading towards the largest of

83

the rocky peaks seen ahead. The trail reduces to a two-wheeled cart track and then to a footpath. Down left views of the Lima Valley suddenly open up.

The path leads to the left, to pass the large ROCKY OUTCROP (**57min**), and you run into sections of old trail again. As you rise to a first crest, a shallow valley is revealed ahead. Cross it by following the path northwest, towards the small saddle ahead. An old trail joins from the left (**1h03min**), and shortly afterwards there is a boggy area to negotiate, before you reach the SADDLE (**1h09min**), where you will find a blue waymark.

Looking just to the left from here, you'll see a small overgrown valley. This was probably the original transhumance route, but ignore it now, and stay with the path and BLUE WAYMARKS, keeping close to the large ROCKY OUTCROP on the right. A smaller outcrop ahead and to the left is reached two minutes later. Follow the path around to the left, and keep left down a mossy gully, to reach the lower end of the overgrown valley (**1h15min**). There are good views now towards Ermida and the trail used in the early part of the walk.

The path continues slightly to the right, to cross the lower end of the overgrown valley. Then it bears around to the left, over rocks. Down on the right now is the deep valley that must be crossed to reach Ermida. The path is way-marked (BLUE DOTS) and fairly obvious, except where it crosses rocks (or where bracken invades). It stays high

up initially, heading in the direction of the distant transmitter masts, before going into a (sometimes steep) zigzag descent. There are boulders to be clambered over at times, requiring some agility, but the path becomes stronger as you descend — eventually widening to a trail.

When you reach the bottom of the valley (**1h24min**), round the bend to cross the STREAM. Two minutes later, descend small steps and head towards another stream. This one is crossed by a BRIDGE (**1h28min**).

From here the trail rises steeply, at least initially, before it divides into a number of paths. At this division keep straight on, to pass a walled-in field on the right, before joining a stone trail again. Dramatic scenery demands attention, especially as you rise

Bilhares summer village (above and left) is reached 36min into the walk. Although basic, it has the essential supply of water throughout the summer (notice the water channels in the foreground). Just behind the village, through a gate, you will find the now-abandoned pastures and fields, enclosed behind granite walls. Top right: beehives near Ermida

and look straight down the Lima Valley (**1h35min**). Ignore a cart track heading left (**1h46min**); keep straight on, to start the descent towards Ermida. You pass some old WATERMILLS near the village. On reaching **Ermida** (**1h53min**), continue through it, to head back to the CEMETERY (**2h**).

Walk 5: BRUFE • CUTELO • CARVALHINHA • CUTELO • CORTINHAS • BRUFE

See also photographs pages 4-5, 21, 71

Distance: 10.5km/6.5mi; 2h46min *(allow 3.5h)*

Grade: moderate, with overall ascents/descents of 350m/ 1150ft. Mostly easy underfoot, on granite trails. The final 100m climb to the summit of Carvalhinha may be omitted.

Equipment: sturdy shoes or boots, long-sleeved shirt, long trousers, sunglasses, suncream, fleece, raingear, picnic, water, *compass*

Transport: 🚗 From Ponte da Barca (note km reading) drive towards Lindoso. After 11km the road drops down to cross a bridge over an inlet of the Touvedo Reservoir. Immediately beyond this bridge turn right (signposted to Germil and Ermida). Pass the café Novas Pontes on your left and come into São Miguel. Turn right by the stone cross (11.2km) and follow a very narrow road up out of the village. At a T-junction (11.8km) turn right and follow

this road through Germil (20.5km), to another T-junction (22.5km). Turn left here, drive past the turning to Cutelo (25km), then follow the signposts into Brufe (27.3km). Park in front of the 'Artesanato' shop.

Short walks: several options; transport and equipment as for the main walk

1 Brufe — Cutelo — Cortinhas — Brufe (4.4km/ 2.7mi; 55min; easy). Follow the main walk to Cutelo. Turn right to the church, then pick up the main walk again at the 2h33min-point.

2 Brufe — Cutelo — watershed — Cutelo — Brufe (5.8km/3.6mi; 1h14min; easy-moderate). Follow the main walk up to the watershed (53min). Instead of taking the same route back to Cutelo, follow the fine granite trail to the right, just as you arrive at the watershed. This will bring you back to Cutelo. From the church, pick up the main walk again at the 2h33min-point.

3 Brufe — Cutelo — watershed — col — Brufe (7.4km/ 4.6mi; 1h28min; easy-moderate). Follow the main walk to the col (just past the 1h05min-point). Here turn right down the shallow valley, making for a grassy patch some two minutes ahead. On reaching this, pick up a path which rapidly becomes a trail contouring round to the right. This will bring you back to the watershed. Now proceed as for Short walk 2 above (from the 53min-point). This version offers fine views on the way up to the col and also back over to Brufe and the mountains beyond on the return leg.

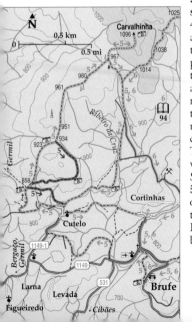

The villages of Cutelo and Cortinhas are literally at the end of the road. So too was Brufe, until 2001, when a road link to Campo do Gerês was opened. As a result these isolated villages experienced even more than others the depopulation of the mid/latter part of the 20th century. This has meant that the villages retain much of their traditional architecture, and the few people remaining to work the land often do so using traditional methods. Historically too, these villages have played important roles in defending Portugal from its Galician neighbours, literally just over the hill. They were also on the contraband routes during the Spanish Civil War and in the mid 20th century. All of this, coupled with some really beautiful and varied country-side, makes this area well worth a visit. But spare a thought for the locals who can suffer weeks on end of fog, gales and drizzle in the dark winter months — probably a very different picture from that which you will see if visiting in the spring or summer! Theirs is a truly hard life which demands our respect as we visit and enjoy seeing the way their work has influenced this delightful landscape over the centuries.

Start the walk in **Brufe** (768m) by continuing along the road (assuming you have entered the village from the Cortinhas direction), passing 'Casa Teifas' on the left. Note the interesting plaque on the wall of the house, which refers

This view opens out as you climb the old trail from Cutelo at the 43min-point. Beyond Cutelo and its pastures there are glimpses of Cortinhas and, in the far distance, the bare granite heights of the Serra do Gerês.

to 'thousands' of refugees who received help here as they entered Portugal during the Second World War. Some 20m/yds further along the road, turn right by a large tree with two gates just behind it. Pass through the right-hand GATE onto a trail bounded by drystone walls. You immediately pass between a large *espigueiro* on the left and a mini one on the right. Continue parallel to and below the road, to cross an old SLAB BRIDGE over a stream (**5min**). Now the trail leads you up to the road. Follow the road to the left, pass the CHURCH on your right, and come to a junction. Turn right here, then go right again immediately, on a track which takes you back down to the stream you just crossed.

The espigueiros at Cutelo (and Cortinhas) are quite unusual in that many of them are built over the trails leading out of the village.

This track rapidly becomes a rough granite trail between drystone walls, leading up into woods. Pass a GATE on your right (**15min**). Four minutes later the trail swings round to the left and rises into some very attractive mixed woodland, with holly, birch, oak and chestnut providing ample shade as well as shelter for a rich variety of bird life. Where trail becomes blocked, take a footpath to the left; this runs parallel to the original trail. Follow this path uphill, then turn right, out of the woodland (**20min**). You cross over a track immediately and descend into a shallow valley. Quickly rejoining a granite trail, you re-enter woodland a minute later. You will shortly glimpse the houses of Cutelo off to the right through the trees.

Ignore a track joining from the left (**27min**) and continue ahead, ignoring a second track on the left three minutes later. Almost immediately you come to a T-junction with a tarmac road (**30min**), where you turn right. Notice the vines supported on wooden posts and tree trunks along here; the local granite is less suitable for fashioning into the slender posts seen elsewhere in the region. The road ends at the entrance to the village of **Cutelo** (750m; **33min**), the lowest point in the walk. Walk on up the granite track into the village, bearing left. *(But for Short walk 1, bear right, to the church.)* Continue uphill until you see a WATER TANK up ahead at the top of the village. Before reaching the tank, notice the WATER TAP on the right. Turn left here, passing under a large *espigueiro*. This

old granite-paved trail rapidly begins to climb up and away from Cutelo, affording fine views across the fields and back down to the village — and to the more distant Brufe. Winding up through pleasant woodland, you pass to the right of a gated track (**41min**). Continue up the granite trail, following intermittent yellow waymarks. Ignore a newly bulldozed track heading up to the right (**46min**); keep straight on, still on the old trail. Almost immediately the route levels off and the granite gives way to an earthen track. One minute later, where the track swings left beside a wall, take the trail leading up to the right (**47min**; there is a rough cairn at this turning). After another minute, when this trail divides, fork right (there is a CAIRN and a YELLOW WAYMARK on the right). Now ignore a path up to the left; immediately beyond it, you will pass a CONCRETE AND IRON CROSS on your left. You quickly reach the top of the ridge (858m; **53min**) — the **watershed between the Lima and Homem rivers**. Straight ahead is a white and red hunting mark on a large rock; immediately in front and slightly to the left is a smaller boulder with a yellow waymark and arrow, which marks the way down to Germil. Ignore this and take the middle route (bearing 070°), which passes just below a huge overhanging boulder a few metres ahead. *(But for Short walk 2, take the trail immediately down to the right. This leads back down to Cutelo, where you rejoin the walk at the 2h33min-point.)* The path divides almost immediately; take the upper

even, on a clear day, to the coast at Viana do Castelo. Look out for Montagu's harriers *(Circus pygargus)* here; in spring and early summer they are often seen gracefully working the hill slopes below.

The granite trail levels off (923m; **1h05min**), and a transmitter mast is visible off to the left. The summit of Carvalhinha is just to the right of it. Follow the level trail for another minute, and you will see an indistinct path leading off right towards a shallow col (spot height 934m on the map). *(Short walk 3 follows this faint path, eventually circling back to the watershed.)*

The main walk continues heading in the direction of Carvalhinha (bearing 060°) and rises to the next shoulder (951m). From here the path begins to swing gently to the left, always with the TRANS-MITTER MAST off to the left. This area is alive with skylarks in spring — just stop and listen if it's a quiet, windless day. The path will lead you into a shallow valley just below a low col to your left (961m; **1h20min**). Now you need to swing right, up the slope on the other side of the valley, aiming for a point just above the TWO LARGE BOULDERS on the skyline. When you reach these boulders, climb the short distance to the top of the shoulder (980m). Now head (060°) towards the highest point of Carvalhinha, passing a

fork, to the left. *(The fork to the right is where Short walk 3 returns to the watershed.)* The path rapidly becomes eroded and (after rain) boggy as it swings round to the left. It is easier to follow the line of the track by walking above and parallel to it for about 75m/yds, then you can return to it where the eroded section ends. The path now becomes a well-defined granite pavement and you can enjoy splendid views out across the terraces of Germil below and the hills above the Lima Valley ... and strangely shaped rock (like a ship's mooring post) on your left. The trail now descends gently into another shallow COL WITH A ROCKY KNOLL IN THE MIDDLE (967m; **1h27min**). You are just below Carvalhinha.

The climb up onto the summit is free navigation from here. Make your way straight up towards the summit initially; then, half-way up, bear round to the right, following a shallow valley. Climb up onto the bare rock to the right of the summit. It is then an easy haul up the final section. The views from the SUMMIT of **Carvalhinha** (1096m/3595ft; **1h42min**) are superb in every direction. If the weather is kind, this is the place to enjoy your packed lunch!

From here retrace your steps to the ROCKY KNOLL (**1h52min**). Now turn due south, down the valley with a large dead tree in it. Head for the tree and then move over to the right-hand side of the valley. Descend for just a minute, then cross over to the left-hand side of the valley, where you will pick up a footpath with yellow and white waymarks and join Walk 6 (**1h55min**). Follow this path down the left-hand side of the valley, then *take care* to follow the waymarks where they guide you back across the stream (**2h08min**). Shortly after this crossing you will come to a track: turn left and then turn right immediately, leaving the track. The way-marks lead you to the right of a ROCKY OUTCROP and then down into a small valley, where you join a major track by a STONE BRIDGE (**2h16min**). Cross the bridge and imme-diately turn left, still following

waymarks. This trail leads you round the hillside, giving fine views out over Brufe. You come into a wooded area (**2h25min**), again on a granite-paved trail. Soon you glimpse Cutelo ahead and below you (**2h31min**). A steep drop brings you down beneath vines; keep ahead, downhill, to reach the WASHING TANK by the route on which you originally left the village.

Walk back down, bearing left, and you will pass **Cutelo** CHURCH (**2h33min**); note the interesting inscription above the door. You then walk under another fine *espigueiro* bridging the trail as it leaves the village (photograph page 88). Walk under vines and, a minute later, where the trail divides, take the lower route. You now wind through pastures and terraces where time has truly stood still. After crossing a small stream (**2h36min**), the main trail drops down into a field ahead; keep left uphill here, on the upper terrace. This path leads round to a STONE STILE. Cross over this and immediately drop down to a stone SLAB BRIDGE (**2h37min**). Cross over and rise up the other side on a granite-cobbled track. This leads you into the village of **Cortinhas**, where you pass a fine group of old *espigueiros* on the left. Walk down through the village and leave it by a modern WATER TANK on the left, bearing round to the right, up to a tarmac road (**2h40min**). Follow this straight ahead, to a junction with a STONE CROSS. Turn left here and follow the road back into **Brufe** (**2h46min**).

Walk 6: BRUFE • CASAROTAS • CHÃ DO SALGUEI-RAL • MARCO DE ANTA • CORTINHAS • BRUFE

See also photographs pages 45, 90

Distance: 10.4km/6.5mi; 2h45min *(allow 4h)*

Grade: moderate-strenuous. There is some stiff climbing, with a height gain of over 400m/1300ft in the first half of the walk. The route is way-marked, but the terrain is rough and exposed. *The way-marks, where they exist, are only visible if the route is done in an anti-clockwise direction. On no account should readers attempt to do this walk in the opposite direction.*

Equipment: sturdy shoes or boots, long-sleeved shirt, long trousers, sunglasses, suncream, fleece, raingear, picnic, water, *compass*

Transport: 🚗 as Walk 5 on page 86

Just in front of the Artesanato shop (worth visiting to see exquisite linen and embroidery, all produced in the village) there is a sign which reads 'In 1706 Brufe did not send men to fight in the war, but defended the homeland from here.' This walk will take you up to the 'front line' of defence that the men from this village patrolled in their constant vigil against their Galician neighbours. You can also explore further on the high ground reached and see an example of a wolf trap, similar to the one shown below.

Start the walk in **Brufe** (768m) by walking down the road towards CORTINHAS. In one minute you reach a bend where the road crosses a stream; immediately after the bridge, turn right on a trail, noting the WHITE AND YELLOW WAYMARK. A minute later bear left by an IRON GATE; the trail continues steadily uphill between drystone walls. In early spring you will find abundant *Narcissus triandrus* sheltered by the walls along this path.

When the trail levels off and a path comes in from the right (**11min**), carry on straight ahead, enjoying the first views to the massive bare expanse of Chã do Salgueiral and our ascent route up ahead. When you come to an open area where several tracks and trails converge (**13min**), turn right

on a dirt track (alongside the drystone wall on the right); there is a WHITE AND YELLOW WAYMARK.

You pass fields bordered by silver birch off to the right. Where the drystone wall swings away to the right (**16min**), take the path straight ahead. The route now becomes a rough path, waymarked and cairned. You reach the first in a series of large, well built CAIRNS (**21min**; photograph overleaf); these mark the route up to the 'front line'. Beyond this cairn you will see a small AQUEDUCT crossing the stream; pass above and to the left of the aqueduct, the path becoming much less distinct now. The waymarks direct you right, to cross the stream (**23min**). As soon as you have crossed, look up to the left, to locate another HUGE CAIRN ON THE SKYLINE. Follow the intermediate waymarks up to this CAIRN (**27min**). From here follow a WATER CHANNEL uphill; after crossing it (**31min**) you will be at the next big CAIRN. Back alongside the water channel (**33min**), shortly you will see the next big cairn on the skyline. Keep following the intermediate waymarks, re-cross the water channel (**36min**) and continue up to this third CAIRN (**47min**). At this point you are

at 999m — at the spot height marked half a kilometre south-southwest of Mata Porcas on the map.

Looking up to the left, the next big cairn can be seen; head for this. The intermediate way-marks now become infrequent, but you can see the next two big cairns, and the transmitter mast also comes into view, so keep heading for these. You reach the LAST OF THE BIG CAIRNS (**1h01min**); beyond and above it is an *abrigo*. Walk to this SHELTER (**1h04min**) and you will find renewed and clearer YELLOW/WHITE WAYMARKING. (Note that the big cairns *do* continue from here round to the highest point on the **Chã do Salgueiral**, but we follow the *painted waymarks* up to the col ahead.)

Follow the waymarks up to the col (**1h12min**), then head round to the right. In another three minutes you will emerge at the first old stone shelters near the SUMMIT of **Casarotas** (1164m/3818ft; **1h15min**). The views from here are truly spectacular. To the southeast you can see down to the reservoir of Vilarinho, with the mountains of Gerês beyond. Ahead are the transmitter masts on Louriça and, behind you, views back down towards the Atlantic. If the air is still, you will hear the calls of skylarks.

Left: seen on Car tour 3, this is perhaps the best preserved and most accessible example of a wolf trap in the region. The Iberian wolf Canis lupus has always been a source of fear and suspicion in these remote hills. Even today people in the smaller villages still avoid going out alone on winters nights for fear of an encounter with 'o lobo'. The lengths to which people would go to try and eliminate wolves were quite remarkable and can still be seen in the form of wolf traps. These consist of two converging stone walls, some 2m/6ft high and several hundred metres long — forming a funnel shape with a pit at the end. The wolf hunters would drive their prey into the open jaws of the trap by making as much noise as possible. The hapless animal would then find no way out of the funnel and eventually be driven into the pit at the end and there killed.

The waymarked route now continues along the ridge towards Louriça. If, *and only if*, the weather is good and you have time, it is worth walking out along this ridge. In about half a kilometre you will come to the wolf trap. Alternatively you may like to walk round to the right and onto the eastern slope of Chã do Salgueiral to find more of the old *abrigos*. Whatever you do, you will afterwards have to retrace your steps to the first shelters at the 1164m viewpoint. Our timings do not include any of the detours possible from this viewpoint.

From Casarotas turn back towards the *SINGLE TRANS-MITTER MAST* in the west. Keep heading across the highest point of the col, aiming slightly to the right of the mast; within two minutes you will pick up white/yellow waymarks on rocks in front of the mast.

These will lead you past the mast and just above it. Then you go through a gap in an old stone wall. Soon (**1h30min**) the waymarks start to become indistinct. They *are* there, but *be careful to locate the next one on the route before moving on.* Now, heading west, pass through another small col (1095m; **1h32min**) and continue on a bearing of 246°. The waymarks lead you to the right (**1h35min**), past a *TOOTH-SHAPED BOULDER* on the crest of the ridge. Here you will get fine views north over to Mézio and Soajo. Then (**1h38min**) drop steeply down from 1075m towards another *COL BELOW THE SUMMIT OF* **Carvalhinha**. From this col (1025m; **1h44min**) the waymarks lead you southwest, heading 210° through another small valley (**1h46min**). You cross over the next shoulder (1038m; **1h49min**), and

Large, well-built cairns mark the route followed by the locals all the way up to the top of Casarotas, seen above in the background.

descend into another valley. Cross the stream in the valley floor (**1h52min**) and follow the waymarks to rise up the other side — to a flat area on the shoulder of the hill (1041m). Locate a SINGLE SMALL ROCK at the top and pick up waymarks leading off to the left (west downhill). Head towards the dead tree down in the valley but, before reaching the tree, the waymarks point you left (**2h01min**), down the valley, at the left-hand side of the stream. (*Walk 5 follows this route.*)

You cross the stream (**2h13min**) and rise to a dirt track a minute later. Follow this track to the left, at this point *leaving the waymarked route (and Walk 5)*. This track takes you over some fairly featureless moorland. Turn left at a T-junction (**2h18min**), to

drop down over a small STREAM. At this point, if you look over to the small hill on the right, you will see some old peat cuttings. After crossing another small stream and walking up the next rise, you will see a small QUARRY (for feldspar and quartz) off to the left. The track swings down to the left (**2h23min**) and then divides; turn right here. The track starts dropping steeply (**2h26min**), passes quartz outcrops on the left, and comes to the corner of a WALLED ENCLOSURE (**2h 28min**). Keeping the wall to your right, you will come down to the junction first reached at the 13min-point. Take the second granite-cobbled track to the right here. This leads you round and above **Cortinhas**. Bear left by some *espigueiros*, to drop down to a T-junction with a tarmac road (**2h35min**). Turn left and left again at the junction with the STONE CROSS (**2h39min**); this will bring you back round to **Brufe** (**2h45min**).

Walk 7: BRANDA DE TRAVANCA • CURRAIS VELHOS • LAGE NEGRA • BICOS • BRANDA DE TRAVANCA

See also photographs on pages 14, 40, 56

Distance: 13.4km/8.3mi; 3h30min *(allow 5h)*

Grade: moderate. There is some 400m/1300ft of climbing to contend with and, while the paths and tracks used are mainly good underfoot, there is a difficult section along a steep hillside which some people might find vertiginous. The highest part of the walk, at 1220m, is very exposed and should be avoided in bad weather/visibility.

Equipment: sturdy shoes or boots, long-sleeved shirt, long trousers, sunglasses, suncream, fleece, raingear, picnic, water, *compass*

Transport: 🚗 Take the road from Ponte da Barca (0km) to Arcos de Valdevez, where you turn right at the first round-about (3.7km), following a brown sign to the national park. Turn right at a T-junction (4.2km) and almost immediately left (green sign to the national park). At 6.3km turn right following signs to Mézio. The road leads into a long steady climb, to reach the national park sign at Mézio (18.5km). Fork left just *before* the sign, on a minor road. Continue past the old campsite and the park's Information Centre on the right. Carry on past the turning left at 20.1 km and keep ahead until the tarmac ends (by a turning up right to the new Travanca campsite; 21.4km). Park in the space opposite this turning.

Short walk: Branda de Cobernos (5.6km/3.5mi; 1h44min; easy; ascent/descent of 320m/1050ft). Follow the main walk to the 52min-point and return the same way.

This circular walk starts off through forest, enjoying comfortable shade and a lovely old granite trail. The first *abrigos* village (see photograph below and caption opposite) passed en route could easily be missed. Built in deep shade and now covered with moss, it blends unobtrusively into the landscape. As the higher altitudes are reached, the forest is left behind, and we

enjoy extensive views over the mountains of the national park. The flora provide plenty of interest along the way, with two narcissi vying for attention in the early summer months — the yellow *N bulbocodium* and the creamy-white *N triandrus*. Also growing in the shady parts is the delicate *Anemone trifólia*, but you will need to be an early spring visitor to see the dog's tooth violet, *Erythronium denscanis*, in flower.

Start the walk at **Branda de Travanca** (789m): take the track up to the right and you will shortly arrive at a fence and gate by the CAMPSITE. Follow the FENCE up to the left and turn right past the top corner (there is *no* proper footpath here). Just round the corner you will see the start of a trail running up the hill. It soon becomes well defined, the huge granite slabs underfoot suggesting that this area was once heavily populated. A steady ascent through woodland follows, where the pink *Silene foetida* lives happily in the cracks of the trail. Views open out briefly to the left (**20min**), where the villages lying on the route of Walk 8 can be seen. A mossy *abrigo* on the left (**26min**; see opposite) alerts you to the *abrigos* village (**Currais Velhos**) secreted nearby, and it is well worth a short diversion up to the right to see it.

Cross a stream (**32min**) and, where the trail divides two minutes later, keep right. As you emerge from the woodlands (**38min**), the trail peters

out and continues as a path for a time, until you reach a wide gap in the wall ahead. Two minutes after passing through the wall there is no path to follow: walk diagonally left, towards the base of a small ridge just beyond a rocky outcrop to the right. As you rise up a little from the wall, the SYMMETRICAL MOUNTAIN PEAK (1292m) above Lage Negra comes into view: head towards it. You join a small path (**45min**) just before reaching the ridge; follow it to the left, onto the crest. Keep on the path, heading down towards the shallow valley ahead, still in the direction of the SYMMETRICAL MOUNTAIN. There is a wet area of springs to negotiate as the path leads you through shrubs, crossing the valley diagonally to the left. Another saddle is reached (**52min**); immediately beyond it lies **Branda de Cobernos** (1114m; photograph page 40), the second village of *abrigos* en route. *(The Short walk returns from here.)*

On arriving at an *abrigo* with a chimney and table outside (the

---

Opposite: abrigos, primitive shelters built from drystone in the shape of an igloo, feature strongly in this walk. They are used by the herdsmen throughout the summer months, when the animals are taken to higher pastures. Often abrigos are grouped together into small villages, sometimes as a loose scattering over the hillside, other times in a tight community incorporating animal pens. On the higher pastures, where there is little shade available, the abrigos are located in exposed positions, but their construction from local stone helps them to blend into the landscape (see also photographs on pages 40 and 56).

one shown on page 40), turn right, to head across the saddle towards the other *abrigos* and the towering mountainside. A short period of free navigation follows from here. Looking to the north, there is a smooth, HUGE GRANITE BOULDER situated on the shoulder, not far below the top — it is a useful landmark. Work your way up the mountainside, aiming to pass immediately above this boulder. You join a faint path just before the boulder is reached (**1h08min**). The path leads you above the boulder and, from here, the path is more easily followed and has CAIRNS. Continue, with the deep valley down on your left, towards the grassy meadow at the head of the valley. At a faint division in the path (**1h10min**), be sure to stay to the left, following the

Relaxing at the summit of Bicos

line of the low wall and gradually descending. Shortly there is another, more shallow valley to cross. As you approach this offshoot of the main valley, the path leads diagonally to the right, through invasive tree heather, and descends to cross a small STREAM (**1h18min**). Follow the path as it rises diagonally left from the stream, towards the meadow and more *abrigos,* reached four minutes later. The path leads out between the last two *abrigos,* heading towards a wall and following the line of the main valley. Shortly, at a division in the path, keep right, to go through a gap in the wall within a minute. The path soon becomes well defined, although invaded by tree heather. Soon (**1h25min**) a track can be seen ahead. Negotiate a wet area and cross a STREAM on the left (**1h27min**). Climb away from the stream over bedrock, following the path first to the left and then to the right, before settling on a course diagonally right — following the line of the stream over to the right. Meet a track in an area called **Lage Negra** (**1h34min**) and turn left.

As you circle the hill on your left, there is a stretch of track-walking for a time, but it gives an opportunity to enjoy the vast panoramic landscapes at this high level (1228m). We have occasionally seen wolves on the higher slopes here, and in the summer months you are likely to see buzzards and golden eagles. When the track swings left (**1h46min**), it is worth making a short diversion to the STONE CAIRN two minutes away to the right at the SUMMIT of **Bicos** (1187m), to delight in the views over this barren and compelling landscape — including Pedrada, the highest point (1416m) in the Peneda section of the national park.

Then return to the track and continue in the same direction but, shortly (**1h54min**), just as the track leads around to the left (and where a ROCKY OUTCROP lies to the right), go diagonally right on a path. (Note that if you were to keep on the track as it leads left, you would eventually come to Branda de Berzavo, cutting about 1km off the walk — but you would miss much of interest!) You join a narrow old granite trail almost immediately. The trail bends to the right, round the rocky outcrop, before descending the hillside. Cross a grassy area (**1h59min**), curving slightly right, to pick up the granite trail again. It soon leads sharply left, affording a wonderful panorama of the valleys, hills, and perched villages surrounded by the terracing that we explore in Walks 8 and 11.

Follow the trail in a zigzag down the mountainside, and note the CIRCULAR WALLED

ENCLOSURE and *abrigo* ahead: the next objective. Go right at a junction (**2h07min**) and turn sharp left a minute later, passing a CAIRN on your right. The trail peters out into stony paths from here, but keep heading for the circular enclosure and *abrigo* previously identified. Reach the CIRCULAR ENCLOSURE and *abrigo* (**2h19min**) and walk round to the left of them; then go left downhill in under a minute, before you reach some rocks. Head down into the shallow valley, to pick up a faint path which soon runs into a grassy trail heading towards pine woods. The trail, now rough and stony underfoot, descends to the right (**2h21min**) and eventually joins a track at **Branda de Bostejões** (**2h28min**). Turn left here, and note the WATER HOLE over to the right; it lies on the route of Walk 8.

There are more *abrigos* up left (**2h33min**), but be sure to turn right onto the grassy track at this point. At the grassy area two minutes later, turn left and take the trail down to and across the river (**Regato dos Bostelinhos; 2h37min**). Climb away on the far side; the trail takes a similar course to the main track, but at a lower level. The trail narrows to a path as it swings left, and the route is not always clear, so be sure to keep to the left of a ROCKY OUTCROP ahead. As you rise up to join an old stone trail (**2h46min**), turn left and rejoin the main track less than a minute later: turn right. Go right at the fork in **Branda de Berzavo** (**3h04min**), and stay with this track as it eventually dips down to cross the bridge over the **Rio Grande** (**3h26min**). There is plenty of leafy shade here, and the pools are an especially tempting place to picnic. From here the track quickly leads back to **Branda de Travanca** (**3h30min**).

Walk 8: BOUÇAS DONAS • BRANDA DE BOSTEJÕES • VITOREIRA • BOSTELINHOS • BOUÇAS DONAS

See also photographs on pages 40, 56 and opposite
Distance: 10.5km/6.6mi; 3h *(allow 4h)*
Grade: moderate-strenuous, with an ascent/descent of about 450m/1475ft. Much of the uphill work is saved for the last half of the walk, with some steep ups and downs to make it more taxing. After the start along a track, the rest of the walk follows paths and trails which are variable, but mainly good underfoot.
Equipment: sturdy shoes or boots, long-sleeved shirt, long trousers, sunglasses, suncream, fleece, raingear, picnic, water
Transport: 🚗 See directions for Walk 7 as far as Mézio (page 96). From Mézio take the turning up past the PNPG Information Centre, then, after 1km, turn left towards Bouças Donas. After 1km the road forks: take the right fork, towards Bostelinhos, and park as near as possible to the top of the rise (immediately beyond a junction, just opposite a circular concrete well on the right).

Short walk: Bouças Donas — — Bostelinhos — Bouças Donas (6.6km/4.1mi; 1h 45min; easy, with an ascent/ descent of 200m/650ft).
Follow the main walk to the 44min-point. Instead of turning right by the rocks, keep ahead and slightly left. Join a trail which takes you out onto a shoulder, keeping to the right of the trig point (849m). You descend the left-hand side of the same valley that the main walk crosses higher up, eventually coming to a major trail junction (just after passing between drystone walls on both sides). The granite pavement is deeply rutted by cart wheels; when these ruts divide into two trails, keep left. In two minutes you descend to the tarmac road at Bostelinhos. Turn left just past the bus shelter, down a steep trail. You join a major track in a minute: turn left and immediately left again, on a trail (opposite a blue-tiled house on the right). Walk down to a bridge, where you pick up the main walk again, at the 2h46min-point.

Variety and points of interest are the highlights of this walk. After an initial climb of almost 200m, you head along the northwest side of a long ridge, before dropping down 450m into the village of Vitoreira. Climbing steadily, the route then follows a line of old villages, as you circle the ridge to return to the start. Vitoreira is typical of many of the isolated villages of the region which rely solely on their own farming efforts for survival. Vines for *vinho verde* are an important crop, as they are throughout the region. In springtime it is always pleasing to see the vines breaking into new leaf, giving a fresh green look to brighten up

Opposite: cultivated terraces below Bouças Donas (Walk 8)

the sombre granite houses and give anticipation for the fruit to come.

We well recall taking this walk with the previous authors, years ago — at the end of September, just at the end of the *vindima* (grape harvest). After an exchange of greetings, one of the villagers of Vitoreira invited us to try his new wine. The traditional bowls *(malgas)* were produced, and these were carefully rinsed with the red wine, before they were filled and passed to us. All our expectations were exceeded, and the wine, rich and deep in colour, was both mellow and fruity, with none of the acidity associated with many 'green wines'. This was achieved, he explained, because they still use the traditional method of pressing the grapes by foot. They had tried a press (he showed us the equipment), but it took too much from the grape, he claimed, leading to increased harshness and acidity in the wine.

The walk starts by the CIRCU-LAR CONCRETE WELL near **Bouças Donas** (709m). Follow the granite-paved trail up the hillside, between drystone walls. After passing through a short section bounded by wire fencing (**8min**), you find yourself back between drystone walls; notice the quartz vein running across the pavement here. Immediately after this, fork right up-hill, still on granite pavement.

The granite trail swings up to the right (**11min**) and a lesser path continues straight ahead. Keep right uphill on the granite trail. In another two minutes this trail breaks out into more open country — still climbing — with fine views off to the south and west. You emerge on a small shoulder (**14min**). The trail swings back round to the left and drops slightly as it passes an ENCLOSURE on the right and crosses a flat green area (full of *Asphodelus lusitanicus* in the spring), once again running between drystone walls. Keep following the line of the wall on the left, now on a less distinct, grassy footpath leading up the hillside.

You pass by a gap in the wall on the left (**17min**), rejoin the wall ahead, and head up towards a rougher drystone wall (**20min**). Walk uphill to the right; while there is no real path for some 20-30m/yds, make your way towards a LONE PINE TREE by some loose stones up ahead. Then, when you meet a forestry track (**21min**), turn left. (Walk 7 follows this track in the opposite direction.)

At a track junction in **Branda de Berzavo** (**26min**; photograph page 56), bear left and cross over a STREAM (**29min**). Continue uphill into pine woods. Here you enjoy expansive views down to the south and west and over the Lima Valley. Nearer at hand, you will see the village of Bostelinhos and part of the route to be followed later in the walk. The track levels off (903m; **34min**). There are enormous beds of asphodels here in the spring, and the woodland now becomes an attractive mix of birch and pine. If you are very quiet and very lucky you might just catch a glimpse of deer in these woods. Usually there is evidence of the presence of wild boar (holes in the ground where they have been rooting).

The track begins to drop gently down and swings round to the left, passing an old FORESTRY HOUSE off to the left (**41min**). As the track swings right, round the shoulder of the hill (**42min**), you will have more fine views. Just below is an old stone enclosure with *abrigos* — another summer village. Soon, as the track heads due north (**44min**), look out ahead for a white quarried scar on the hillside ahead. When you see this, look down to the left, below the track, and you will find a path leading down left

Thatched barn and haystacks at Vitoreira

towards *A PAIR OF ROCKS FORMING A PYRAMID* (just 20m/yds below the track. Walk down to this 'pyramid' and then, directly in line with the quarry scar, turn right on a faint path, down into a small hollow. *(But for the Short walk, keep ahead here.)* The path rapidly becomes a more distinct trail and leads you down into a valley, where you cross a STREAM (**51min**). Although there is no shade,

this is a delightful spot to stop and cool your feet in the rock pools, while taking in the views of the summit of Bicos (Walk 7) and the hills leading to Pedrada, the highest point in the Peneda section of the national park.

Cross the stream and head diagonally left uphill, to continue on the trail. In two minutes you rise to a grassy track at **Branda de Bostejões**. Turn left here, heading for the

OLD QUARRY workings. Turn left just past the quarry (by a red and white hunting sign; (**55min**).

Head up the slope on an initially indistinct path and, at the top of the rise, walk between some rough boundary stones, keeping the first hilltop on your right. You should by now see the ALVITE TRIG POINT ahead in the distance. Continue ahead as a grassy trail joins from left (**1h06min**), and

follow the trail as it heads diagonally to the right. Walk between rocky outcrops, to the other flank of the ridge. When you come upon STANDING BOUNDARY STONES, keep them on your right. Walk down the middle of a GRASSY AREA (**1h11min**), to find the continuation of the trail, and follow it slightly left — towards the trig point, which is again in view. This is a good area for spotting foxes. Shortly (**1h14min**) a good granite trail comes underfoot and, as you climb this section, eventually passing below the **Alvite** TRIG POINT, you can enjoy good views down over the valley to the right.

Keep right, downhill, at the fork (**1h26min**). The trail leads to the left almost at once, to continue along the ridge, now descending a little. As you near the end of the ridge, the trail becomes vague, especially as you approach an area of flat bedrock (**1h38min**) with a rocky outcrop beyond it. Go diagonally to the left of the outcrop to pick up a good trail again within two minutes. Head left to cross the end of the ridge. Keep on the old trail, to meet a wall on your right (**1h42min**) and cross a stream almost immediately. Turn right on the far side of the stream and follow the line of the wall, passing in front and to the left of a PYLON. The trail ascends slightly now, before starting its descent off the ridge.

Stay with the trail as a path forks off right (**1h45min**). As you swing to the left here, you catch the first glimpse of Vitoreira ahead. Turn right at a T-junction (**1h47min**) and follow this trail round the

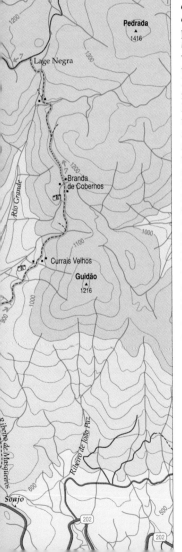

rocky outcrops, curving to the left as you descend. Keep left at a fork (**1h57min**). Still descending, keep left, ignoring paths off to the right. Three minutes later a sprinkling of red-roofed farmhouses, interspersed with haystacks and *espigueiros* can be seen below. Turn left to follow the walled-in cobbled track through the village of **Vitoreira**, sometimes walking beneath vine-covered pergolas. Keep right at a fork (**2h05min**), to reach a SLAB BRIDGE (436m) over the stream four minutes later.

Cross to the right. Shortly (**2h11min**), as you rise away from the stream, leave the trail: take a path climbing the hill to the left. Soon it is bounded by walls on both sides. Keep ahead as you rise up to crest the hill, and ignore all paths joining the one you are on. Terraced fields are soon encountered (**2h24min**) and, shortly afterwards, there are glimpses of the next village en route. You will get fine views down to the Ribeiro de Vilela below and, if you have

binoculars, try looking for otters.

Now on a wider trail, the climbing becomes quite stiff for a while. Be sure to head around to the left, when a trail departs to the right (**2h30min**). But two minutes later, when the trail again bends around to the left, turn right on a minor trail, soon passing a SPRING on the left. **Bostelinhos** comes into view up to the left now, and you pass to the left of its POST OFFICE (**2h39min**). A minute later, turn left between houses (the trail ahead soon runs into a track). You quickly pick up the old trail again, on the right, opposite a blue-tiled house. It descends steeply, affording views of the terraces shown on page 100, to cross the stream by a METAL BRIDGE (**2h46min**), then climbs the far side of the valley — just as steeply. Turn left at the 'T' of trails one minute beyond the bridge and zigzag up to the next junction (reached six minutes later), where you keep left. Now under a pergola of vines, you look down to the right over the valley, to see cultivated fields, old houses and more *espigueiros*. Keep heading upwards through the village of **Bouças Donas** (**2h54min**). Continue climbing by going left at the fork two minutes later, to pass a CHURCH down to the right. Keep ahead almost immediately, as another trail crosses diagonally. Turn right as you rise up, to meet a track two minutes later, and go left when you join the road from Bostelinhos, to find your car by the CIRCULAR CONCRETE WELL (**3h**).

Walk 9: SOAJO • BRANDA DA BORDENÇA • ADRÃO • BOGALHEIRA • RIO ADRÃO • SOAJO

See also photo pages 16-17
Distance: 12.8km/8mi; 3h59min *(allow 5h)*
Grade: moderate; over varied terrain. Most of the ascent, on good tracks and trails, occurs in the first half (a height gain of 350m/1150ft to Adrão). After Bogalheira, navigation on the open hillsides becomes more difficult, and this section should not be attempted in poor visibility.
Equipment: sturdy shoes or boots, long-sleeved shirt, long trousers, sunglasses, suncream, fleece, raingear, picnic, water, *compass*
Transport: 🚗 follow Car tour 3 (pages 35-37) to the *espigueiros* in Soajo. Park here.
Shorter walks: four landmarks en route make good turning points if you wish to shorten the walk. All these are a slightly easier grade than the main walk, but they all still involve some climbing. Equipment as for the main walk.
1 Casa Abrigo — Branda da Bordença — Adrão — Bogalheira — Casa Abrigo (8.6km/5.4mi; 2h10min). To park, turn left off the road between

Mézio and Soajo, taking the road signposted 'Peneda, Casa Abrigo'. Park 6.3km along this road, by the forestry house on the right (Casa Abrigo). Start the walk by following the path down the right-hand side of the house. It goes left round the back of the house and becomes a trail. In 2min it meets the route of the main walk, which joins here from the right (at the 1h07min-point). Keep ahead, to follow the main walk to Adrão and return the same way.
2 Soajo — Casa Abrigo — Soajo (7.9km/4.9mi; 2h14min). Follow the main walk to the Casa Abrigo (fine views); return the same way.
3 Soajo — Branda da Bordença — Soajo (9.6km/6.0mi; 2h40min). Follow the main walk for 1h20min; return the same way.
4 Soajo — Branda da Bordença — Senhora da Paz — Soajo (10.6km/6.6mi; 3h04min). Follow the main walk to Senhora da Paz (1h32min; refreshments available in summer). Return the same way.

Many old cobbled trails lead from Soajo, providing access for the villagers to the lands that they farm. The trail we join was built by the Cistercian monks to link their monastery at Ermelo with another at Fiães (near Melgaço). Following the trail initially, passing several watermills along the way, the walk takes you beyond Soajo, to visit the now-uninhabited village of Branda da Bordença, where many of the granite houses stand largely intact and where there is an old toll house by the bridge on the monks' route. Adrão is the next landmark en route; it boasts a small bar (summer only). From here the walk leads downhill, crosses the head of a huge valley, and goes on to another deserted village, Bogalheira. From here we climb gently up to Alto das

Cortelhas and then, on open hillside with splendid views down to Soajo and the Rio Adrão below, finally drop down to the river and back to the *espigueiros* in Soajo.

Start the walk at **Soajo** (300m): cross the road from the *espigueiros* and take the small trail opposite, turning right then left to come up into the village square shown on page 112 (**2min**). Turn right in the square, taking the granite pavement to the right of the CHURCH. Turn left behind the church, almost immediately passing the BAKERY on your left and then the POST OFFICE on your right. Bear left at the next junction (**5min**) and shortly after pass 'Casa Laranjeira' on your right. At a T-junction (**6min**), with TWO GREEN GATES ahead, turn left on a granite pavement. At the next T-junction (**7min**) turn right, rising gently up to a small square with a WATER TAP opposite.

Take the track just to the left of the water tap, heading uphill out of the square. Look out for an old WATERMILL on the right. Just beyond the watermill (**8min**), turn right on a lesser stone-cobbled track (there is a modern house with concrete steps alongside the start of this track). This track quickly becomes a major cobbled trail, finally heading up and away from the village.

Views of the neatly terraced steep hillsides down to the right distract you for a time, as you climb steadily, ignoring trails off first to the left and then to the right. As the trail leads round to the left (**16min**), there is a particularly fine view back over Soajo. WATERMILLS come into focus next: there is a line of them on

the left, reached a minute later, as you round the bend to the right. Stay on the main trail, still climbing, to reach a small DAM (**28min**) which provides the head of water to run the watermills below. Pass to the right of the dam and, three minutes later, cross a lovely old SLAB BRIDGE over the stream. On the far side, turn left. You are now on a stabilised track, which you follow as it takes a winding course up the hillside, ignoring minor trails off to the left. Signs of cultivation gradually disappear and the landscape becomes barren for a time, particularly around the **46min**-point. Noticeable here on this heather-covered hillside is the small pink heather, *Erica umbellata*.

On the crest of a rise (**47min**), take the waymarked path heading up to the right, following the line of the wall on the right. Notice, as you rise up, the TRIG POINT ahead, on top of an interesting mound of rocks. Your path is now a well-established trail. In another two minutes you come to a T-junction with a track, where there is a stone wall on the far side. *(For Shorter walk 2, take this track to the left and, when you reach the road, turn right to the Casa Abrigo, a further two minutes away. Then retrace your steps to return.)* Turn right at this T-junction (**59min**), with the wall on your left, breaking away from the track and following the wall round to the left almost immediately. When the wall ends (**1h02min**), walk diagonally left towards the woods; the trig point at Branda de Murça is now on your right. Follow the line of the valley and head straight towards the deserted granite village of Branda da Bordença, which blends so well into the

The walk starts from alongside the espigueiros *at Soajo. They are grouped on top of a granite hillock and have a central drying space* (eira), *which is also used for flailing. Skilfully sculptured and meticulously constructed with interlocking joints, many of these stores have survived for two centuries. They stand on mushroom-shaped stilts to deter rodents, since they are used to store* espigas *(maize which is grown on the terraced hillsides). At harvest time, the maize is gathered and brought to the* eira. *After drying, the grain is ground to flour, usually in a watermill of which there are many in the village, and used to make a maize-flour bread called* broa. *The long stalks from the maize plant have a use, too: they are stacked together in the fields, like hay, and used as winter litter in the cow sheds. See also 'Agriculture and landscape', pages 69-73.*

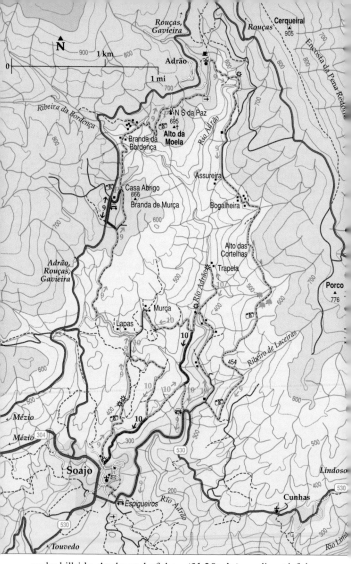

rocky hillside. At the end of the woodland another trail joins you from the left (**1h07min**); follow this to the right. *(Shorter walk 1 joins here).* Keep heading towards the deserted village; you reach a delightful old bridge over the **Ribeira da Bordença** ten minutes later. The building on the right is the old TOLL-HOUSE. The main trail bypasses **Branda da Bordença**

(**1h20min**), so divert left here to explore it.

Then continue up the trail, to emerge opposite the church of **Nossa Senhora da Paz** (662m; **1h32min**; Picnic 12). Keep ahead over the open grassy area at the left of the church, to continue on an old walled-in trail with YELLOW WAYMARKS. Follow this trail to the CEMETERY on the right, where you meet the bend of a

The abandoned village of Branda da Bordença blends perfectly into the granite landscape. Note also the drystone walls and the granite trail in the photograph, typical of so many walks in the area.

cobbled road (**1h39min**). Keep ahead here, to descend into the village of Adrão. Views of the terraced hillsides across the valley to the right catch the eye as, walking beneath vines, you finally enter **Adrão**. By a WHITE AND RED WATER HYDRANT (**1h44min**), turn sharp right on a minor trail (between yellow waymarks). (Or first continue ahead to find the small seasonal café.) The trail leads down towards a gate a minute later. From here follow a walled-in path to the right, descending steadily through very peaceful

111

The main square at Soajo, with the pillory in the centre. The pillory is topped by this unusual stone triangle and, strangely, a happy-looking face.

rises up to a track). Turn left uphill just above an almost-concealed red-roofed house (**2h05min**). Almost immediately, when you join a grassy track above the house, turn right. Shortly you will join an old granite trail, which takes you above **Assureira** and on into the (almost) deserted village of **Bogalheira** (546m; **2h12min**). At the time of writing, there was still one lone inhabitant in the village. He had been born there, emigrated to America and then France and had finally returned to the place of his birth, to end his days, solitary but content to be there.

Head through the village under trellises of vines, and turn left uphill, to walk past an *espigueiro* and between two buildings above it. You immediately come to a T-junction in the trail (**2h14min**); turn right here, to leave the village and walk above it, passing a couple of *espigueiros* on the right. The rough trail continues alongside

countryside. Keep down left at a junction (**1h49min**): in two minutes you come to a picturesque WATERMILL in a natural beauty spot. An old bridge spans the gurgling water, and mossy rocks and lush vegetation enrich the green of the encroaching woodland ... an irresistible resting place.

After crossing the bridge, continue along the path, now starting to ascend. Soon you leave the woodland behind (**1h55min**) for open countryside. As the path forks (**2h03min**), keep ahead on the lower fork (the left fork quickly a drystone wall until you come to a small STREAM crossing (**2h19min**). Carry on round, still with the wall on your right until the wall starts losing height (**2h22min**) and the path leads left uphill, away from the wall. In another minute, when the path divides, take the upper route — up to the rocky promontory of **Alto das Cortelhas** (591m; **2h26min**).

Just after the top of this rise you will come to a drystone wall with a gate in it; walk to the left, keeping the wall on your right. The path now becomes quite faint, and some care is needed with navigation. The views will tempt you to forget navigating — but pay close attention to the notes below!

Where the wall swings away down to the right, look ahead and you will see TWO PINE TREES. Head for these and, on reaching them, look ahead to the next shoulder, which has another, SINGLE PINE TREE on it. Head slightly above this tree, towards a DISTINCTIVE BOULDER a little upslope. When you reach the boulder (**2h29min**) look ahead, due south, to the next hillside, where you will see a large COPSE OF SILVER BIRCH TREES with some old terraces up behind it. Aim for that birch copse. The path is faint, but if you keep heading for the copse you will descend into a valley with a stream crossing just in front of the copse. Cross the STREAM (**2h38min**), walk up into the copse, and pick up a more distinct path through and out of the trees. This will bring you up to another ROCKY PROMONTORY (**2h42min**) with fine views out over Soajo and

the Touvedo Reservoir beyond it.

From here drop down across a shallow valley towards PINE TREES. Just below and to the right of the trees you will find a path (**2h46min**) leading down the hill exactly in the direction of Soajo (bearing 230°). Very soon you will see a road bridge far below. Just in front of this bridge, you should see a small round hill with a distinct path running round and in front of it. We have to join this path and it requires some free navigation over the open hillside to get there.

When you reach the path on the SMALL HILL (454m; **3h03min**) follow it round and down into the next valley, to cross a STREAM (**3h16min**). Then contour round the next hillside on a well-defined path. Navigate a short stretch of fallen broom (**3h25min**) and then come into eucalyptus woods. There are beautiful views down to the waterfalls and pools in the **Rio Adrão** from here. As you emerge from the eucalyptus (**3h28min**), look for a path off down to the right between drystone walls. Follow this steeply downhill, to a fork (**3h34min**). Turn right and in another couple of minutes you will come down to a track, where you turn left. This track brings you to the ROAD BRIDGE seen previously (**3h42min**). Cross over and then follow the road 1.7km back uphill to the *espigueiros* at **Soajo** (**3h59min**).

See also photographs on pages 38, 108-109, 112
Distance: 8.1km/5mi; 2h29min *(allow over 3h)*
Grade: moderate. There is an altitude gain of some 250m/ 820ft, mostly on the climb from the river Adrão up to Murça. Some rough narrow paths in the first part, easy underfoot on tracks and trails in the second half.
Equipment: sturdy shoes or boots, long-sleeved shirt, long trousers, sunglasses, suncream, fleece, raingear, picnic, water, *compass*
Transport: 🚗 follow Car tour 3 (pages 35-37) to the *espigueiros* in Soajo. Drive on from the *espigueiros* for another 1.7km, until you come to a bridge by a U-bend. Park here.
Shorter walks
1 Soajo — Trapela — Soajo (4.0km/2.5mi; 1h28min; easy-moderate). This option cuts out much of the steep climbing, but still gives a good flavour of the walk. Follow the main walk

for the first 44min, until you reach the old hamlet of Trapela, then return the same way.
2 Soajo — Rio Adrão — *espigueiros* (5.4km/3.4mi; 1h35min; easy; includes some road-walking). Follow the main walk to reach the Rio Adrão (35min). Cross the river and follow the trail leading up to the left. Continue ahead (41min; the main walk turns right here at its 58min-point) and follow the trail back towards Soajo. A simple bridge of slabs is crossed (48min); three minutes later, keep straight ahead. Ignore the trail joining from the right (1h02min). You enter Soajo opposite a house with '1923' on the wall (1h15min). Go to the left of this house, and turn left almost immediately. Keep right at two junctions, to reach the square. Take the exit at the left of the pillory and come to the main road. Turn left, and keep left past the *espigueiros,* to get back to your car (1h35min).

S oajo is a fascinating and thriving village which attracts visitors — particularly to see the *espigueiros,* the granite-built grain stores shown on pages 108-109, which are imposingly grouped together around an open area of rock (used as a threshing and drying floor). It is worth a stop as you drive past to see them. This circular walk explores the steep valley running north from where the car is parked and down which flows the river Adrão. Scenic interest is not lacking at any stage. Heading first up the left bank, a small abandoned hamlet is visited, before the river is crossed on stepping-stones. There is a long climb up the other side of the valley to the farming community of Murça. Careful navigation through the maze of trails surrounding Soajo is needed to get back to the car.

Start the walk at the BRIDGE (235 m) 1.7km northeast of **Soajo**: continue along the road and cross the bridge over the

Rio Adrão. Then turn left immediately, to join a rough track. There is a steep ascent to tackle straight away — and over stony ground. Stay with the track as it briefly narrows to a trail and passes just above a small BARN (**4min**). Just after this you will rejoin the track as it passes through woodland and crosses a STREAM (**11min**). A short steep ascent follows, and the track swings sharply uphill to the right. Take the path off to the left on this bend (**18min**) — the track itself ends abruptly. The path takes you down through a cluster of old buildings now used as ANIMAL PENS and approaches the river three minutes later. Turn right at the junction of paths here, to climb the hillside again; then keep ahead (**24min**), ignoring the path joining from the right. You

The river Adrão and the old terraces and fields near Trapela

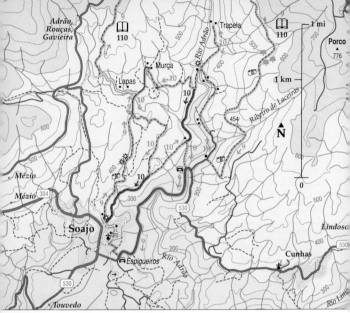

Waterfall and pools at the Rio Adrão river crossing, first reached in 35min

will need to step over a low wall across the path a minute later, just as you reach a small building on the right. Beyond this point the path becomes a little overgrown, especially as you approach another small building (**31min**). The path passes to the right of this building, then leads you into a winding descent towards the river. Farmed terraces across the valley and a watermill and an old farmstead by the riverside catch the eye, as you descend to reach the **Rio Adrão** (**35min**) at the setting shown above.

This will be our crossing point, but first we make a short excursion to Trapela, further along the valley. Continue along the riverside, to pick up the path again. It leads you back up the hillside, and soon you are looking down over still-farmed terraces surrounding the old hamlet of **Trapela** (shown on pages 38 and 115). As you arrive by the river (**44min**), there is an old WATERMILL up to the right. Follow the path down alongside the river for a further minute, to reach a shaded arbour — a natural beauty spot where you might choose to picnic (but watch out for water snakes). Don't cross the river here, but go back to the crossing point referred to above, which you first reached in 35min. You are now **52min** into the walk.

Cross the river, which can be flowing fast in spring, on stones. Head for the trail opposite, by the farmhouse (if the trail is blocked with wire netting you can easily climb into the field on the left and then rejoin the path a short way ahead through a gate). Continue as the trail immediately leads you into a steady climb, with the valley on your left, until you reach the crest of this rise (**58min**). Turn right by a RED AND YELLOW WAY-MARK, to enter an old walled-in trail, climbing steeply again and bearing left (**1h01min**; *no* waymark). Three minutes later, after the trail takes a sharp right-hand bend (waymarked), you're facing the head of the valley. Shortly afterwards (**1h06min**) the trail ends at a wall. Clamber over the wall to continue diagonally left along a path which joins a rough trail two minutes later; follow this to the left. Looking across the valley from here you can see Trapela and, further along, the old granite village of Bogalheira which is visited in Walk 9.

As you approach the cultivated terraces of **Murça** (**1h11min**), the route narrows to a walled-in trail. At a junction of trails reached two minutes later, turn right (waymarked). There is a whole network of walled-in trails around Murça, but navigation is easy. *Ignoring* the waymark indicating left, keep ahead on the granite-paved trail (**1h14min**), to reach a major junction of trails three minutes later. Turn left here, passing a WATER SOURCE on the left. Ignore the two trails heading right (**1h20min**), but turn left immediately afterwards on a broad improved track. This will lead you to a stone SLAB BRIDGE (also on the route of Walk 9). Cross to the

left and join a track (**1h25min**). In two minutes you emerge in a wide open area with a small DAM, where the track becomes a trail. Don't go straight on along the main trail (it leads back to Soajo), but take the smaller walled-in trail heading diagonally left. Soon (**1h30min**) it takes you to another open area. The inclination is to stay with the trail as it swings right towards Soajo, but it is important to *leave* this trail. Cross this open area, following the wall round to the left, and join a trail leading *away* from Soajo and back up the valley (at least initially). Follow the trail as it swings sharply down to the right three minutes later (in front of a small IRON GATE in the wall ahead of you). Continue down to a 'T' of trails (**1h36min**), where you turn right, follow a narrow walled-in trail. There are glimpses of the road below, as you enter woodland. Ignore the trail joining from the right (**1h43min**) but, as you join a main trail two minutes later, turn sharp left: set your back on Soajo once again and start heading up the valley. Continue ahead for a time, crossing a WATER CHANNEL, until you meet a trail which leads sharply back downhill to the right (**1h54min**). This trail, which would quickly takes you down to the road where your car is parked, has become almost impassable. The alternative is to continue ahead, where you will rejoin the outward leg of the walk at the 58min-point. Turn right downhill here, retrace your steps back across the river and down to the BRIDGE 1.7km northeast of **Soajo** (**2h29min**).

The Celtic influence is still to be seen in the old granite round houses, as illustrated here, just before the 1h32min-point in the walk. An old Celtic settlement can be visited near Viana do Castelo: see Picnic 3 and the plan on pages 130-131.

down the trail to the right (**1h32min**; just beyond where the photograph above was taken). At the fork just over a minute later, turn down right and, at the T-junction which is soon reached, go left. A narrow walled-in trail takes you down to a good granite track (**1h37min**), where you turn left to continue. (*Alternative circuit 1 joins from the right here.*) In four minutes you meet a tarmac road: bear right. Soon

look for one last short cut: just before you reach a walled-in ENCLOSURE on the right (**1h52min**), go down to an old trail on the right and follow it, keeping the wall on your right. Cross a stream two minutes later and rejoin the road (**1h59min**). Go straight on to return to your car at the SHRINE outside **Vilar** (**2h10min**).

Walk 12: CIRCUIT OF PENAMEDA FROM NOSSA SENHORA DA PENEDA

See also photographs on pages 42, 44
Distance: 8.6km/5.3mi; 2h34min *(allow 3.5h)*
Grade: moderate-strenuous, with over 400m/1300ft of ascent in the first half. There is a very steep descent at the end on granite pavement and steps. Mostly waymarked.
Equipment: sturdy shoes or boots, long-sleeved shirt, long trousers, sunglasses, suncream, fleece, raingear, picnic, water
Transport: 🚗 follow Car tour 3, turning left towards Peneda at 20.6km and rejoining the tour notes at the 28km-point as described on pages 36-37. Continue following the tour as far as the 48km-point (page 42), when you will be at the sanctuary of Nossa Senhora da Peneda. Park here.

T his walk offers the contrast between the Peneda sanctuary, Nossa Senhora da Peneda, with its associated trinket shops and cafés (especially busy in the first week of September during the annual pilgrimage) and spectacular mountain and upland scenery — just a couple of kilometres in distance, but worlds apart in atmosphere. The sanctuary itself owes its origin to the legend of an apparition in the 11th century, when a young shepherdess had a vision of a dove and then 'Our Lady'. The villagers were sceptical, but then an ailing local was miraculously cured at the same spot.

Start the walk from alongside **Nossa Senhora da Peneda** (686m), just above the CEMETERY: walk back north along the road, in the direction of LAMAS DE MOURO. At a T-junction, you pass the road bridge over the **Tieras River** (**6min**). Continue north on the road, passing a blue 'P' sign on

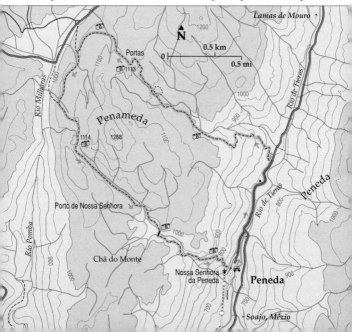

The sanctuary at Peneda is by no means small — as can be seen in the photograph on page 44. Nevertheless it is dwarfed by the huge rock face behind it (left). We start the walk from this sanctuary and the return leg brings us down alongside dramatic cliffs, from where we enjoy fine views over the village (above).

There follows a stiff ascent of 350m/1150ft, mostly on a fine granite pavement. As a brief respite, the path levels off (**42min**), then drops slightly to a small stream. But it soon rises again through sparse oak woods. The path levels off again (**48min**), and the awesome rocky scenery ahead begins to come into view. Soon the huge cliffs of **Penameda** loom off to the left. You pass a small ENCLOSURE on the right (**56min**).

Go through a small gate (**1h04min**), making sure to close it behind you. Now the path becomes more faint — but it *is* cairned. You walk over granite that has been smoothed by glacial action and finally reach the first pass — **Portas** (1113m; **1h07min**). From here there are splendid views off to the south. Keep a look out for buzzards and the odd

the left and a national park sign on the right (**15min**). Just after passing a RUIN on the left, you will find another blue 'P' sign on the left (**18min**); there is a NATIONAL PARK SIGN indicating this waymarked walk. Turn in here. You pass a concrete WATER TANK and, just behind it, there is a sign showing the walk route.

eagle. You will probably find plenty of evidence of 'snufflings' of wild boars here as well.

The path continues as a sandy surface until you regain a granite trail (**1h09min**). This crosses a small stream via a concrete CULVERT (**1h13min**). From here there are fine views northwest over to the isolated hamlet of Bouça dos Homems. Soon (**1h18min**) the trail becomes much clearer and is running parallel to the road 60m below.

Take care to strike off left, *leaving* the granite trail where it turns sharp right down towards the road (**1h21min**). On this bend there is the start of a faint footpath, with CAIRNS. Within a minute or two this becomes a more distinct, granite-paved footpath, quite overgrown in places, but cairned. It rises steadily. When the path levels off (**1h29min**) follow the cairns towards the narrow cleft on the skyline, reached three minutes later. Where a path joins from the right (**1h34min**), turn left uphill towards the next gully on the skyline. In two minutes you reach a granite pavement again and pass through the gully (spot height 1114m on the map; **1h40min**). From here you have extensive views to the south and get your first glimpse of a reservoir below.

The path is now clear and well defined, leading down the valley towards the water. After descending into broom, heather, holly and oak, full of bird life, bear slightly left (**1h55min**), following the cairns to cross the STREAM a minute later.

As you skirt round the edge of the RESERVOIR (**1h59min**), you will doubtless hear the continual 'plop' as frogs jump in. Notice too the marsh and wetland plants, particularly *Eriophorum angustifolium*. The grassy banks overlooking the reservoir make a peaceful picnic spot, and if you sit quietly here for a time, you will usually be rewarded with a sighting of birds of prey high above.

Cross over the small DAM (**2h02min**); you may need to paddle if the water is flowing over the top. Then turn left, following the CAIRNS down the right-hand side of the valley. The path drops down left towards the stream (**2h05min**), and the stream is eventually crossed on a stone SLAB BRIDGE (**2h11min**). The Peneda Valley to the south now begins to open out below, and you start a steep descent on granite pavement and steps, dropping down into mimosa woods through which you can glimpse the twin towers of the sanctuary (**2h30min**). Four minutes later you will drop down to the car park alongside **Nossa Senhora da Peneda** (**2h34min**).

BUS TIMETABLES

Viana do Castelo — Ponte de Lima — Ponte da Barca — Arcos de Valdevez

	b		a	a	b		b	
Viana (Central)	7:20	8:20	9:50	10:10	11:50	12:20	13:20	13:50
Viana (Marina)	7:30	8:30	10:00	10:20	12:00	12:30	13:30	14:00
Darque	7:40	8:40	10:10	10:30	12:10	12:40	13:40	14:10
Deão	7:50	8:50	10:20	10:40	12:20	12:50	13:50	14:20
Geraz do Lima	7:55	8:55	10:25	10:45	12:25	12:55	13:55	14:25
Vitorino das Donas	8:00	9:00	10:30	10:50	12:30	13:00	14:00	14:30
Ponte de Lima	8:15	9:15	10:45	11:05	12:45	13:15	14:15	14:45
Refoios						13:05		14:35
Tavora						13:25		14:55
Gandra	8:35					13:35		
Ponte da Barca	8:55					13:55		
Arcos de Valdevez	9:05				13:45	14:05	15:15	

a	Except Saturdays, Sundays and national holidays
b	Except Sundays and national holidays
c	Except Saturdays

Arcos de Valdevez — Ponte da Barca — Ponte de Lima — Viana do Castelo

	b	a	a		b		a	c
Arcos de Valdevez					7:10	7:20	8:50	9:10
Ponte da Barca					7:20		9:00	9:20
Gandra					7:40		9:20	9:40
Tavora						7:40		
Refoios						8:00		
Ponte de Lima	6:10	6:45	7:15	7:30	8:00	8:20	9:30	10:00
Vitorino das Donas	6:25	7:00	7:30	7:45	8:15	8:35	9:45	10:15
Geraz do Lima	6:30	7:05	7:35	7:50	8:20	8:40	9:50	10:20
Deão	6:35	7:10	7:40	7:55	8:25	8:45	9:55	10:25
Darque	6:45	7:20	7:50	8:05	8:35	8:55	10:05	10:35
Viana (Marina)	6:55	7:30	8:10	8:10	8:40	9:05	10:15	10:40
Viana (Central)	7:05	7:40	8:20	8:20	8:50	9:15	10:25	10:50

a	Except Saturdays, Sundays and national holidays
b	Except Sundays and national holidays
c	Except Saturdays

a		b	a	a		c			
15:35	15:55	16:35	17:15	17:35	17:50	17:50	18:20	19:45	19:50
15:45	16:05	16:45	17:25	17:45	18:00	18:00	18:30	19:55	20:00
15:55	16:15	16:55	17:35	17:55	18:10	18:10	18:40	20:05	20:10
16:05	16:25	17:05	17:45	18:05	18:20	18:20	18:50	20:15	20:20
16:10	16:30	17:10	17:50	18:10	18:25	18:25	18:55	20:20	20:25
16:15	16:35	17:15	17:55	18:15	18:30	18:30	19:00	20:25	20:30
16:30	16:50	17:30	18:10	18:30	18:45	18:45	19:15	20:40	20:45
	17:10				19:05				
	17:30				19:25				
		17:50			19:05				
		18:10			19:25				
	17:50	18:20			19:45	19:35			

a	b			a	b	a		
	10:20	12:00	13:10		16:10		18:00	18:00
			13:20		16:20		18:10	
			13:40		16:40		18:30	
	10:40	12:20						18:20
	11:00	12:40						18:40
10:45	11:20	13:00	14:00	15:00	17:00	18:00	19:00	19:00
11:00	11:35	13:15	14:15	15:15	17:15	18:15	19:15	19:15
11:05	11:40	13:20	14:20	15:20	17:20	18:20	19:20	19:20
11:10	11:45	13:25	14:25	15:25	17:25	18:25	19:25	19:25
11:20	11:55	13:35	14:35	15:35	17:35	18:35	19:35	19:35
11:30	12:05	13:45	14:45	15:45	17:45	18:45	19:45	19:45
11:40	12:15	13:55	14:55	15:55	17:55	18:55	19:55	19:55

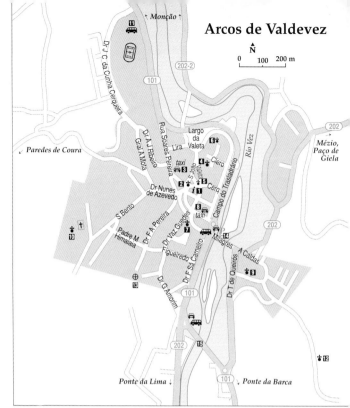

Ponte de Lima

1. Tourist office
2. Main church
3. Misericórdia church
4. Senhora da Penha de França chapel
5. Post office
6. Bus station
7. Car parks
8. Nossa Senhora da Guia church
9. Hospital
10. Santo António chapel
11. Anjo da Guarda chapel
12. Porciras e Escadarias chapel
13. Pillory
14. São Francisco e Santo António dos Capuchos church
15. Old bridge
16. New bridge

Ponte da Barca

1. Tourist information offices
2. Main church
3. Misericórdia church
4. Town hall
5. Health centres
6. Post office
7. São Bartolomeu chapel
8. Santo António chapel
9. Medieval bridge
10. Roman bridge
11. Pillory
12. Old market

Arcos de Valdevez

1. Tourist office
2. Nossa Senhora da Lapa church
3. Taxi rank
4. Main church
5. Nossa Senhora da Conceição chapel
6. Espírito Santo church
7. Misericórdia church and cross
8. Taxi rank
9. São Paio church and staircase
10. São Bento church and convent
11. Bus depot
12. Remédios chapel
13. Hospital
14. Old bridge
15. New bridge

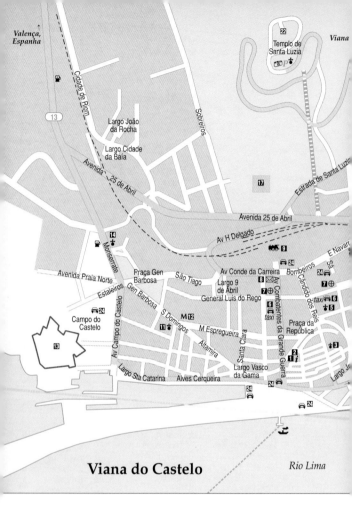

Viana do Castelo

1. Tourist office
2. Old hospital
3. Sé (Cathedral)
4. Malheiras chapel
5. Misericórdia church
6. Taxi ranks
7. Medical centres
8. Post office
9. Railway station
10. Almas church
11. Santa Cruz church
12. Municipal museum
13. Santiago da Barra castle
14. Senhora de Agonia church

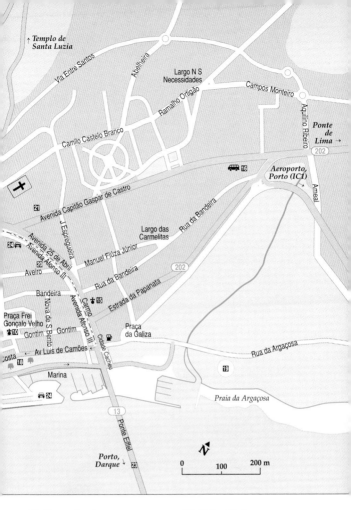

15 Carmo church
16 Bus station
17 Hospital
18 Public gardens
19 Bull ring
20 Police station
21 Municipal market

22 Celtic village
23 Two-tier iron traffic and railway
   bridge
24 Car parks

Braga

N

0   100   200 m

#		#	
1	Tourist office	7	Railway station
2	Sé (Cathedral)	8	Hospital (São Marcos)
3	Santa Barbara gardens and Archbishop's palace	9	Police
4	Praça do Comercio	10	Post office
5	Car parking	11	Library
6	Bus station	12	Town hall
		13	Biscainhos museum/gardens

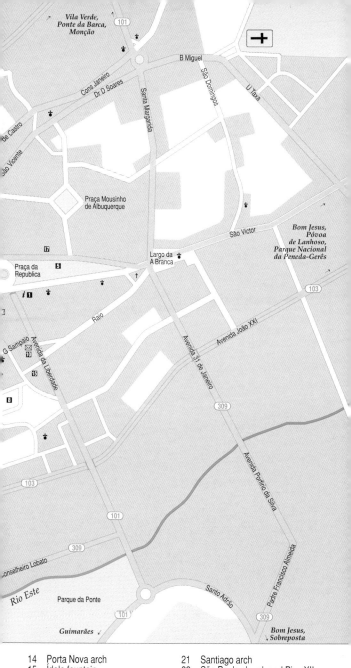

14	Porta Nova arch	21	Santiago arch
15	Ídolo fountain	22	São Paulo church and Pius XII museum
16	Menagem tower		
17	Nogueira da Silva house/museum	23	Regional museum
18	Crivos house	24	Roman archaeology foundation
19	Coimbras house and chapel	---	approximate line of Medieval city walls
20	Sacred art museum		

Index

Geographical names comprise the only entries in this Index; for other entries, see Contents, page 3. **Bold-face page numbers** indicate a photograph; *italic page numbers* a map; both may be in addition to a text reference on the same page. To help with pronunciation, accented syllables are printed in bold; underlining indicates that the vowel should be slightly nasalized.